So You Are… PREGNANT!

By Stephanie Rae

Illustrations Matthew Garrity

I acknowledge the Australian Aboriginal and Torres Strait Islander peoples of this nation. I acknowledge the traditional custodians of the lands on which I am privillaged to author. I pay my respects to ancestors and Elders, past and present and am committed to honouring Australian Aboriginal and Torres Strait Islander peoples' unique cultural and spiritual relationships to the land, waters and seas and their rich contribution to society.

Disclaimer: The material in this publication is of the nature of general comment only and does not represent professional advice. It is not intended to provide specific guidance for particular circumstances and it should not be relied on as the basis for any decision to take action or not take action on any matter which it covers. Readers should obtain professional advice where appropriate, before making any such decision. To the maximum extent permitted by law, the author and publisher disclaim all responsibility and liability to any person, arising directly or indirectly from any person taking or not taking action based on the information in this publication. This is a work of creative non-fiction. The views expressed are the author's own. The events and retellings portrayed are not word for word, but as accurate to the best of the author's memory. Names, dates, events and locations have been changed, removed and/or fictionalised to protect the identity and privacy of all involved. Many parts have been fictionalised in varying degrees, for various purposes. For example; in some cases events have been compressed or fictionalised (the latter for humour only), and certain characters are a combination of two or more people, or an embellished representation of real situations encountered.

THIS BOOK IS DEDICATED TO

My Children
The most patient beings I probably don't deserve who thankfully inherited more than just my crazy.

Green Man
Without you none of this would have been possible... or so funny.

Kathryn & to all the happy-go-lucky Kathryns out there
You were one of the first people I shared this tale with & I think you would've laughed at the book version as joyously as you did all those years ago. RIP my friend.

PLEASE BE ADVISED

Adult content, language and subject matter.

So You Are Pregnant is not recommended for younger readers.

For all you foul mouthed over 18s – enjoy!

NOTE TO MY NAN

(… and anybody else's Nan)

Sorry about the swearing.

SO YOU ARE… PREGNANT!

Is a self-guided story.

It is not to be read from beginning to end.

Follow the options at the bottom of each page

If you get lost go to – *from page…* to retrace your steps.

As with most things in life, surprises may arise

(like bub's gender changing half way through your journey)

You can either retrace or embrace!

All lead to the same hilarious and dysfunctional outcomes!

CONTENTS

(if you get completely lost)

Goodluck ☺

ONE EARLY MORNING…

PART 1: YOU ARE PREGNANT

SO IT BEGINS

PAGE 1: CONGRATULATIONS!

PAGE 2: A COLD BLOODY DOWNER

PAGE 3: A) DEMAND SHE CEASE!

PAGE 4: IT'S A GIRL

PAGE 5: A) WHO WILL DRIVE?

PAGE 6: TENNIS BALL SNIFFING WEIRDO

PAGE 7: HE DOES!

PAGE 8: B) POSTPONE

PAGE 9: TIME TO GO HOME

PAGE 10: WRAP IT UP

PAGE 11: B) HAIRY LITTLE OVERCOOKED WOMB LOVER

PAGE 12: A) HEADS: C-SECTION

PAGE 13: THE CAR BACK STORY

PAGE 14: BABY SHOWER

PAGE 15: B) GO OUT

PAGE 16: A) SLOW DOWN

PAGE 17: CRAVINGS AND HABITS

PAGE 18: A) A DAY OUT

PAGE 19: A) FALL INTO A HEAP

PAGE 20: A) TAKE GREEN MAN

PAGE 21: A) IMMEDIATELY STARTS RESEARCHING

PAGE 22: THE PARTY

PAGE 23: BEDRIDDEN

PAGE 24: THE MIDWITCH

PAGE 25: B) WALKING THE DOG

PAGE 26: B) RECLAIM YOUR BREASTS

PAGE 27: A) THE FOOD HALL

PAGE 28: A) WAG IT

PAGE 29: CANDLE LIT DINNER

PAGE 30: GREEN MAN GIVES MAN-CHILD A BATH

PAGE 31: WEDDINGS, PARTIES, BIRTHS

PAGE 32: PART 2 – THE MIDDLE

PAGE 33: WELCOME TO THE MIDDLE

PAGE 34: VISITING HOUR FROM HELL

PAGE 35: SOLDIER ON

PAGE 36: GO HOME

PAGE 37: THE NURSERY IS DONE!

PAGE 38: ELEPHANT BABY

PAGE 39: B) LOSE YOUR BANANA

PAGE 40: B) PULL UP YOUR BIG GIRL PANTS

PAGE 41: B) LET HIM GO

PAGE 42: OVERACHIEVING NONG

PAGE 43: B) BABY SHOPPING

PAGE 44: CONGRATS ON 12 WEEKS

PAGE 45: PARKING AT THE HOSPITAL

PAGE 46: DRIVE YOURSELF TO HOSPITAL

PAGE 47: B) PRIVATE HOSPITAL

PAGE 48: COOCHIE COO – WHO'S A SEXY PRAM?

PAGE 49: PRIVATE HOSPITAL HOTEL

PAGE 50: PART 3 – THE FINALE

PAGE 51: ROLL UP ROLL UP

PAGE 52: B) BESTIE WITH A BABY

PAGE 53: THE WHITE COATS OF CHRISTMAS PRESENT

PAGE 54: CAREER CALAMITY

PAGE 55: THE THIRD DAY TIT

PAGE 56: THE BIRTH PLAN

PAGE 57: B) SOBRIETY

PAGE 58: A CHANGE OF PLANS

PAGE 59: BESTIE TO THE RESCUE

PAGE 60: A) WAIT FOR ASSISTANCE

PAGE 61: B) DISTRACTIONS

PAGE 62: SEX

PAGE 63: B) SLEEP IT OFF

PAGE 64: B) KEEP WAFFLING

PAGE 65: B) CUE BESTIE

PAGE 66: B) BITCH SLAP YO SELF

PAGE 67: IT IS TIME TO GO

PAGE 68: THE BABY EXPO

PAGE 69: A) SOURCE CHOCOLATE

PAGE 70: BABY GIRL IS COMING

PAGE 71: A) BEERPALOOZA

PAGE 72: NO HOMECOMING FOR BABY

PAGE 73: A) RECENTLY GIVEN BIRTH POSTAL

PAGE 74: B) HEAD HOME

PAGE 75: A) BACK TO BUB

PAGE 76: ALL ABOARD/DOWN WITH THE SHIP

PAGE 77: SUPERDICK HAS SOME ANNOYING SUPER POWERS

PAGE 78: B) SIT BACK AND RELAX

PAGE 79: B) TAILS: MIRACLE ON CAESAREAN STREET

PAGE 80: THE UNFINISHED BABY ROOM

PAGE 81: A) CALL BESTIE

PAGE 82: THE DRUNKEN HUSBAND

PAGE 83: B) AQUA AEROBICS

PAGE 84: A) TELL HIM STRAIGHT AWAY

PAGE 85: SAVE VS SPEND

PAGE 86: WILL THIS BABY EVER COME OUT?

PAGE 87: A) RELEASE THE BEASTS

PAGE 88: A) HOSPITAL CAFETERIA

PAGE 89: B) BACK ROAD

PAGE 90: PART 4 – DISS-FUNCTION

PAGE 91: HERE COMES THE BABY

PAGE 92: B) A LESS RATIONAL APPROACH

PAGE 93: A) MATERNITY SHOPPING

PAGE 94: A) FRESH GODDESS

PAGE 95: PRE-NATAL CLASSES

PAGE 96: A) GO TO LUNCH

PAGE 97: B) BUZZ FOR ASSISTANCE

PAGE 98: B) YOUR OVERPRICED WELLBEING

PAGE 99: A) PACK UP YOUR SHIT

PAGE 100: A) ZOMBIE APOCALYPSE POSTAL

PAGE 101: WAITING FOR RESULTS

PAGE 102: A) GREEN MAN'S WELLBEING

PAGE 103: B) CALL A TAXI

PAGE 104: B) THE SHOWER/SHAVE DILEMMA

PAGE 105: B) THE FREEWAY

PAGE 106: A) PUBLIC HOSPITAL

PAGE 107: TIME TO GIVE BIRTH

PAGE 108: A) CHILD FREE BESTIES

PAGE 109: SPRINT TO THE EXIT

PAGE 110: CHRISTMAS MORNING AND STILL NO BABY

INTERVAL: CELEBRITY HEADS WITH NAN – OR AM I A CHOOK? (MENTAL HEALTH NAN-BREAK)

PAGE 111: A) CALM

PAGE 112: RETREAT THE BEASTS

PAGE 113: WHY SUPERDICK? JUST WHY?

PAGE 114: FINALLY BRING BUB HOME

... THE BLOODY LONG BEGINNING

MUMMING

HOME LIFE

MIDWITCH 2ND STRIKES AGAIN -OR- ARE YOU EFFING SERIOUS?

REUNION WITH THE WORLD'S BEST MIDWIFE -OR- THE GREATEST SILVER LINING OF ALL

A WORD FROM GREEN MAN

CONGRATS YOU MADE IT TO THE END!

THANKS & ACKNOWLEDGEMENTS

BIO

ONE EARLY MORNING...

One early morning as the world slept, my infant son and I were tucked up in the spare room feeding and reading. In between the trials and angst of vampire love – I reflected on my own time of being a baby maker. Nobody would believe such a bizarre story, but with any luck the tale would give people a laugh and reassurance that they are not alone. A book I wish I had during all that joyful craziness, but also during times of confusion, isolation and sadness. Of course it would be a roaring success, get picked up by a streaming channel and a hottie cast as my husband. I would reluctantly play myself (*note: insert multiple snogging scenes*).

Let's be honest Mums – from woe to go on the journey of pregnancy (and beyond) some crazy crap goes down. Most of the time we're in mashed-banana-brain mode questioning if any of it actually happened.

I've often used my birth stories as a party favorites and thought why not share this extremely personal and rather ridiculous account of what seemed to be one shenanigan after another – with the world!

So You Are... Pregnant! is a light-hearted romp with a few heart-stringy moments for anyone who is pregnant, has ever been pregnant, or is planning on the venture. Enjoy whilst sprawled out restless from hours of trying to manoeuvre a heavy belly into a position that doesn't make you want to pee! For the reluctant night owl at 2:30 in the morn – boob on the bed, dusting crumbs off bubs bald spot from a late-night snack you've whipped up to replenish the insatiable hunger of being a 24/7 walking udder. For the 3.5 minute moments you get to yourself – usually on the loo and even that's not sacred. Or at the four billionth appointment you and bub need to attend. Or those tiny rare seconds where the planets align and all is silent and still in the world to read a few chapters. Bahahahahahaha! Yeah right. This is not a fantasy novel. Regardless when you find the time – this joy generator is for you.

This is also for the Dads and Partners at our side. The Men and Women accompanying us on our journey along with the Mothers, Fathers, Grandmothers, Grandfathers, Sisters, Brothers, Aunts, Uncles, Cousins, Friends and support units in all their glorious forms.

While this is a book about pregnancy, it's also about being human. To those who have boldly chosen not to have children, bravely dealing with not being able to, who aren't ready, or are struggling in any way – this book is for all of you too.

Finally, for Mums at all stages –YOU– unbelievably powerful, beautiful and amazing YOU are at the forefront of my mind as I pen these words. Exhausted and deliriously baby-loved-up being, who is probably wounded, but hopefully healing. Confused, but making your way through the cloud. What you just did, or are about to do is nothing short of a bullshit miracle – no matter how your bundle has arrived, or is arriving into the world. If you are a newbie, or a seasoned pro – take this moment to acknowledge that every single pregnancy and birth – no matter if it's your first or fifteenth – is a phenomenal act and you deserve a whole lotta light, love and nurturing. I see you. I was you. I've clicked send and comic relief should arrive via a chuckle very soon.

Most of this book touches on personal issues, stories, thoughts and themes based on actual events with a very fictional twist. A *How Not To* if you will. I have purposefully not researched current trends as I didn't want them to influence what was and still is my journey and the takeaways you may (or may not) receive. I have modernised some parts (ie tech references), but it is a fairly genuine account of my first pregnancy and bits of my second.

In the name of story flow and to protect significant others and so I don't have to write Dear Husband, or Hubby, or DH, or any other annoying crap every time, I refer to the Father of our children as Green Man – in honour of his hideous drunken colour and the fertility deity.

In my story, I refer to people who give birth as: Mothers, Mums, Women and breastfeeding Mums/Mothers as this was based on my journey and a different space in time. I hope this doesn't negatively impact anyone's reading experience and please know you are seen, heard and valued as is your journey.

I hope you enjoy my tale and if you don't... well, I hope you can chill and just scroll on.

#lesssaltymoresweetie #lessjudgymorefudgy #kindnessishot

PART 1
YOU ARE PREGNANT

SO IT BEGINS

Three months ago you got married. Yay. Congrats. It was a beautiful ceremony with loved ones and much twinkling. The whole wedding thing only came about as you had been with your partner for seven years and were excited to dive into the next chapter of starting a little family. Hubby to be was not so keen. But the tick-tock of your biological clock beat ever louder and it seemed everywhere you looked friends, colleagues, randoms were entering that stage of their lives and seemed deliriously happy. You wanted a slice.

The engagement ring sat in his jock drawer for over a year. You would take it out and picture all the fanciful dreams about your wedding day and how when he finally did put a ring on it – life was going to be a magical dream (cue canned laughter). You reasoned seven years was a fair innings and called bullshit on his "I'll ask when I'm ready" spiel. It's not that you desperately needed to get married before kids. This was more of a sympathetic extension for his procrastinating wankery. You were never one to put forth ultimatums (he would flat out ignore them anyway), but you reasoned it was time. So you gave him a choice – get married or start trying for a baby. For one of THE biggest putter-offerers on the planet there was no confusion in his answer.

"Get married," he blurted.

"What? Really?"

"Yep."

"Okay. Wow. Awesome," you gushed at the sliver of romance and that was that.

So marriage it was and he dodged a bullet for ten months during the wedding madness. What he didn't count on was his titanium sperm and your severely fertile eggery would successfully unite the second you stopped contraception. According to the boastful Green Man he was born to feed, while you were born to breed and fall pregnant almost immediately. Much merriment ensues, though Green Man would only jump on board the baby joy train once he met his son.

Before your husband earns the *Green Man* title, he is a perpetual tone of grey for the duration of your pregnancy, donning multiple shades way before it becomes a reference for kinky sex. For nine months he shapeshifts in and out of a petrified pallet resembling all the freaked out colours of having a kid. He wallows in a turmoil tornado of becoming a Dad and the lamentation of frequent sex. Having sex is not an issue for you – wanting to vomit on him when a morning sickness wave hits mid-thrust is your main conundrum.

All this penis pining prepares you for things to come – much sighing and an obscenely inappropriate level of alcohol consumption by a non-drinker in parent denial.

And so it begins…

GO TO: PAGE 1

PAGE 1: CONGRATULATIONS

You come home from your fifth trip to the shops and head straight to the bathroom. Let the toilet contortion begin! You dance the ritual dance of prime, pregnancy-stick soaking without weeing on your hand. Well done. Cups are for amateurs and probably ladies, though you've abandoned any hope of becoming *belle of the ball* at this point. You've mastered pregnancy kits in a matter of days, which wasn't that hard considering this is the seven hundredth time you've tested. There is a graveyard of plastic sticks piled up around your feet. You may have gone slightly overboard. By your calculations you should have seen two pink lines, two hours, four minutes and thirty three seconds ago. You are yet to appreciate the fun world where things like clocks and watches are no longer relevant. Your body and the sabotaging little squirmer inside are here to shut that whole time thing right down. You work off their schedule now. You are their bitch.

You don't bother busying yourself for the three minute wait time. You stand over that thing like a hungry hound watching as the tiny little tsunami stains the white beyond.

One pink line... it's too much! You close half an eyelid and turn to flush the toilet. Two pink lines... whoa... hang on...

YAY! YOU ARE PREGNANT! LET THE JOURNEY BEGIN!

Still in shock, you do a few glory laps around the house with much woo-hooing, fist pumping and a couple of ear-piercing screeches.

Your screams of delight ring like a house alarm to a heavy-footed neighbour who begins hauling himself over the fence with something resembling a machete.

"Hang on love… I'm comin!" he calls out like a grizzly bear dangerously close to snagging his manhood.

"It's alright. I'm okay," you call back like a high-pitched chipmunk.

"Bloody hell! Thought I was gonna have to punch on in me jocks! You okay?"

"Um… well… yes! Actually, I just found out I'm pregnant!"

"Oh, that's fCking fantastic! Just wonderful love! Congrats to ya both!"

You soon realise you've shared the most important news of your life with a machete-wielding, possible drug-dealing neighbour. You run to get the phone and ring your significant other.

**DO YOU:
A) TELL HIM STRAIGHT AWAY: PAGE 84
B) POSTPONE: PAGE 8**

PAGE 2:
A COLD BLOODY DOWNER

(from page 79)

Well done! You WARRIOR! What a full on twenty four hours that was! Still groggy from the whole affair you look around a room you've been pushed into. For the first time in a long time you're alone. Bub is next to you in a little crib and all you want to do is hold him, but there's still lots of wires and tubes and you can't feel your legs. He sleeps soundly all gooey and swollen, so you put your head back on the pillow and wait for the Midwives to check in. And you wait. And you wait some more. The door is ajar and you can see the shadows of people running past. Nobody seems to be coming to check on you. This must be normal. Just *standard procedure*, you reason. You look at the button and decide not to press it. You don't want to seem demanding, though your reluctance to offend the staff is not the best plan of action right now as everything starts to wear off. You can feel the sensation of your parts coming back and with it the pain. But, there is something else happening under the covers and it feels weird. You pull the stiffened sheets aside. You are still lying in blood and there's a lot of it. It's pooling up both sides of your legs. You grimace and put the covers back.

DO YOU:
A) WAIT FOR ASSISTANCE: PAGE 60
B) BUZZ FOR ASSISTANCE: PAGE 97

PAGE 3:
A) DEMAND SHE CEASE!

(from page 24 & 26)

This is demented! You manage to locate her hand and push it firmly away.

"Enough! He's choking!"

"He is not. He just doesn't know how to breathe through his nose. He needs to learn to latch or you're going to have problems," she scoffs.

"I'll figure it out," you snap back. You've officially gone postal.

The *midwitch* is still for a moment and you wonder if she is going to counterattack, or has realised the severity of her actions. You have your elbow stuck out like a Roman spear aimed and ready just in case, but she launches around it.

"Well, you'll need to express, anyway. You can hold him on one breast and express the other. You need to learn now rather than trying at home without help," she orders, emotionless.

You shake your head in disbelief and imagine what actual help would look like, but there's no time to follow that thought. She yanks hard at your boob again and attaches the horrible contraption to your poor, poor breast. She flicks a switch. The shock takes hold as you hang your head in defeat and just let it happen. Better you than the baby. The room fills with noise and you feel some form of relief – at least physically.

"How does that feel?" she asks, daring to give a shit. You can't make eye contact. Your baby is still screaming hysterically from the ordeal and you try to soothe him best you can with half of your body twisted and contorted. Everything is beyond your control. The sheer frustration that you are exposed in every way in front of this masochist brings on the waterworks – another thing you have no control over. You can barely breathe and to any normal human with a pulse it would be obvious you are struggling on multiple levels. But, the *midwitch*'s humanity is questionable, and she offers no comfort at all. You feel hopeless and just want her to go away.

"Fine. I'd like to be alone now."

"He's still not latching and he won't in that state. Give him to me and I'll settle him in the hall," she says reaching in like a child-snatching monster and every instinct in your DNA seems to come alive. You all but snarl at her.

"No!" you raise your voice and this time it's you doing the thrusting. You shield your child with one hand and hold up the other at her. "*I* will settle him. We just need to be on our own now, thank you," you order.

Her eyes are wild and you have no idea what she'll unleash next, but you are done. You look toward the door. She stands defiantly over the bed. You are no longer taking her bullying bullshit and deliver her a death stare that champions every Mother who has ever been messed with. Well, maybe not so dramatic. Thankfully, she slinks out of the room and never returns. Oddly, your brain chooses to lock *this* memory in a very deep, dark vault for many years.

After she leaves you monumentally break down. The shock, the pain and the disbelief of witnessing your child's first experience of fear and feeling powerless to stop it finally hits you. Bub still screams while you cry so hard you can barely catch your breath as your right boob continues to be a prisoner of the electrical sucking arsehole. You have no clue how to turn it off, or even if someone will be back to help and just as the tidal wave of crap seems like it could not possibly get any more traumatic – your bosses walk in on the lot. Of course they fecking they do.

GO TO: PAGE 34

PAGE 4:
IT'S A GIRL

(from page 65)

Eating copious amounts of chocolate is thirsty work and as per your usual methods of preparing for ultrasounds – you get a little eager with the water guzzling. You make a petrol station pit stop and purchase a 1.5L bottle. You are adamant to drink the exact required amount to avoid mishaps. You fill up your pretty 'Mummy' bottle bought specifically for this moment and sip away in the waiting room with Bestie. You've timed everything perfectly and gloat that your brain is capable of calculating anything at all. You're a lifetime subscriber of arithmophobia and the whole *baby brain* thing ate the last bit of your mathematical ability. Ta ta's. As you stare at the many bellies surrounding you at the reception area, memories flood of childhood math struggles.

SHIT MATH SKILLS FLASHBACK

Your long-suffering Father could not comprehend your non-comprehension of even the most basic mathematical principles. As your zombie-glazed face stared back at him, Daddy dearest – ever the anti-calm presence – executed some less than curriculum approved homework methods. With his butcher's cleaver, chopping block and a soon to be brutalised orange – learning about fractions was less than a passive affair.

"Okay. Again. **These** *are fractions. Tell me what this is?"*

"An orange?"

"A whole... (breathes way too deeply) this is a bloody whole! Now if I cut it in two, what do we have?" He brought the cleaver down so hard it shook the lime green breakfast bar down to its cement foundations. Your reluctance to answer was no surprise.

"Ummm... two oranges?" you asked, still clueless. You just wanted a slice of orange.

"Oh, for shits sakes. NO. Half! Two halves. Never mind. If I cut them again, how many do we have?" he asked with a wobble in his voice as the knife carved a crater into the chopping board. Even at eight years of age you knew you were doomed.

"Uummm..... urrr.... four?"

As a little girl your Dad seemed like a giant man. What was even more giant was his moustache. That thing had a life force of its own and at times could be a multiple personality moustachio, twitching in time with his eyeball. It seemed like Andre the giant and Tom Selleck's love child was standing before you, armed and crazed.

"There... are... (twitch) four... (twitch twitch) pieces of orange... yes... but... (combo twitch) what fractions have they been cut into now (disco twitch)?"

"Ummm.... I forget. What are fractions again?"

Luckily your Mum walked in before a mo-snapple-dapple went down.

"What's with the knife?" she questioned, raising her own brow.

"I'm helping her with math homework."

"With a meat cleaver?"

"You have a go then. We're up to quarters, eighths are next and she's just asked what fractions are. Good luck," sung Dad way too *eagerly as he skipped to the fridge, grabbed a six pack of Swan Gold, cracked open a tinny and skulled it before he was four paces away. Three hours later Mum had passed out from the bottle of wine required to get her through the ordeal. You had oranges for dinner. There were many. Ironically fractions would sink in when you got a job on the Pizza Hut chopping line. Suddenly it all made sense. Pizza – the greatest teacher – reigns supreme. Always.*

***

Back to the water...

Alas, math evades you again. You've overestimated your intake. There's more liquid than baby and the ultrasound lady is unimpressed by all your squirming.

"Go and relieve a little, Mrs Man," she orders and rolls her eyes. You give an embarrassed nod and run the gauntlet to the dunny, typically miles away and wonder how in the veritable fCk you are going to clam up mid-piss? Bestie follows you in and is still giggling. She actually tried to defend your stupidity to the technician. True love even when you've massively muffed up the actual muff.

"Think tight thoughts," she suggests as you release a few dribbles.

"Right."

"Sucking on a lemon."

"Okay."

A few drips drop.

"Sticking your finger into those sea urchin thingies,"

"Good one."

Bit of a trickle.

"Venus flytrap."

"Nice."

More of a pour now.

"Nup!"

You're losing it.

"Clams!"

"Here it comes," you cry out as the carefully procured urine is literally pissing your hopes down the toilet.

"Finding out the sex of your baby!" she yells back and you clench down hard with every ounce of vaginal strength you possess, which considering your children are yet to butcher your little ole-lady-hooie – is still a malleable powerhouse.

"Yes! That did it!"

"Yay!" Bestie does a little celebration dance before you both exit triumphantly and struddle back to the ultrasound room.

"Welcome back, Mrs Man and... Mrs Man?"

"Of course," you respond without skipping a beat and immediately take Besties hand. You grin. She blushes and for this moment you are officially unofficially married and it's funny-as to see her squirm knowing she can't back out now. Being your wife isn't the issue. It's her inability to lie. She is the world's worse liar – testament to her angel awesomeness.

"Okay. Let's see what the lucky couple are going to be having," says the technician as she lubes you up with warm goo and begins probing. It is here in this very normal, average procedure that things became confusing and forever more remain a mystery to you, Bestie and probably the ultrasound lady. She was either speaking in tongues, or the two of you had a surge of subliminal stupidness where you both mistook the same thing that you have no idea if it did or did not actually occur. It certainly would not be the first, nor the last time Twiddly Dumb and Twiddler Dumber would strike.

SONOGRAPHER: Something, something, something... *describing limbs and other stuff she sees... more waffle... something... ah... a boy...* something, something...

Bestie throws you a split second bit of sympathy. She knows, despite your anti-ovary campaign – you really did want a little Bumbalina.

YOU: Aww a little boy. Cool.

BESTIE: Naww a boy. Yay.

SONOGRAPHER: Sorry ladies. What are you talking about?

YOU: It's a boy. Yay. Yes?

SONOGRAPHER: Um, no. You're having a girl, Mrs Man's.

YOU: What? Really? I thought you said a boy? Holy crap! Really?

SONOGRAPHER: *looks at you both like you are mad and smiles.* Really. No boy. This is a beautiful clear image of a baby girl. See.

You both look over at the scratchy, gloopy black-and-white picture of your little miss and it suddenly seems very feminine. You imagine blobby in a tutu and can't wait to braid her hair, paint her nails, climb trees and take her fishing.

Bestie gives you a huge hug. There is much joy, tears and elation. You can't stop smiling and wonder if the sonographer is waiting for a more intimate celebration from you both. You giggle and wiggle your tongue through your fingers at Bestie who immediately begins choking. Oblivious, the technician congratulates you both as more giggling ensues. You throw Bestie a wink and cross your fingers this lovely lady never sees you with Green Man. That could get tricky.

Back in the car you pour half a bag of celebratory chocolate bullets down your gullet and grab the phone. Around the same time unusual tremor waves are reported across several continents. It has scientists stumped, but not you. You know the exact culprit.

"Hi, Mum."

"Oh, stop with the niceties and tell me! What you are you having?"

"Okay. Well…"

"Yes.…"

"It's…"

"C'mon!"

"a…"

"It's a girl!!!!! Aaaaaaaaahhhhhhhhhhhhhhh!!! I bloody knew it!! Aaaaaaaahhhhhhhhhhh!"

"… girl."

You take the phone off speaker. Even with the windows up and the engine running, people passing by jump with shock. You laugh and leave her to her to it. She immediately starts ringing her entire contact list and posts pink back screens onto Facebook with *I'M GOING TO HAVE A GRANDDAUGHTER!* and #blessedgranny and other proud grandparent hashtags.

You, however are starting to relate to her long-suffering OMS – Overlooked Mother Syndrome. Your neglectorino Mum notoriously became invisible as her mother accosted and mauled her grandbabies with gooing and gaaing and many a *"That's Nanny's girl/boy"* while her daughters would stand in the doorway babyless, without so much as a peck on the cheek. Allegedly.

You are happy for your Mum to have this moment. Lord knows the woman deserves a win after decades of uncertainty of not only where you'd end up, but if babies would ever be on the cards.

"Oh… and how are you, love? How are you feeling?"

"I'm all good, Mum. Got a bag of chocolate bullets and I'm going home to rest."

"Yes, you do that. Take care of my granddaughter please. Eat a vegetable."

"I will."

"Oh, I'm so happy! A little girl! And I'm happy for you too, of course!"

"Of course," you reply and just when you think you've escaped it…

"… and I can't *wait* to see how much trouble she causes you! Payback baby!" There it is. Mum's vengeance. She has a point. You went from angelic cherub to crazed wildling for a decade or so. In her eyes it's the natural order of things for you to cop a bit of what you dealt. And you will. You are in for a whole lot of copping with your little Bumbalina-to-be. But that's a booze-soaked worry for another day.

Now you know what you're having, time for some fun. Grab wifey! It's Baby e**X**po time!

GO TO: PAGE 68

PAGE 5:
A) WHO WILL DRIVE?

(from page 67)

Congratulations! It's you! This comedy of errors somehow groups together to finally leave the house. It's a few days before Christmas, so madness is everywhere and you'd rather avoid *Methy-The-Snow-Nosed-Reindeer and Co* if you can. Though Mother dearest still proclaims her sober innocence – everyone agrees better safe than sorry. Or in your case – better safe than giving birth in a filthy jail cell with *Biffo-Barbara* warming up the stirrups and *Off-Chop-Charlie* pinging near your nethers. Mum's out.

Then there's Green Man – who from this moment on officially earns his title. He is GREEN in every sense of the word. It's not a pleasant forest green, more like a sludgy vomit shade. The type you might find at the bottom of a swamp, or the pit of a dead animal's stomach, or ironically the shade of baby shit. He manages to dress and spew twice in the process. The first vom is in the ensuite sink. Yummo. You are so high on happy hormones you not only laugh as you discover it, but actually clean the high-level repulsion up. The last time you saw chunder that chunky was on the first day of your first ever job at the Royal Show.

FIRST VOMIT-CLEAN JOB FLASH BACK

A kid had just been on the Mighty Mouse and thought mowing down a hamburger with the lot and an extra-large red creaming soda straight after, was a smart thing to do. It wasn't and five seconds later he proceeded to hurl it across the diner's floor all ruby-red and steaming. The spotty 'manager' handed you a mop and grinned.

"All yours newbie."

Arsehole. Ironically, it was inside a massive hamburger. You were quietly elated when they bulldozed it to the ground many years later.

You laugh at the memory forgetting it for another decade and remember you are actually in labour.

Back to the chundering Father-to-be...

The second time Green Man vomits is as you all make your way to the brand spanking new car. This will not only be the first time you have driven, but have been allowed in it at all. Green Man has probably never been this drunk in his entire life and will most likely never again go through a life-changing experience as huge as this. But, even amidst this mile-stoney glory and the putrid state of the situation – OCD is the all-ruling, carry over champ. The perfect state of Green Man's car trumps the minor issue of hastily getting a birthy, messy wife with her leaky, ooziness safely to hospital. No sir! Not on his hideous, vomit dripping watch!

More flashback montaging – though this thing requires a page of its own.

GO TO: PAGE 13

PAGE 6:
TENNIS BALL SNIFFING WEIRDO

(from page 40)

Eventually the cravings subside replaced by more peculiar fixations – like tennis balls. Not eating them, but sniffing them. Yes. Go you. You discover this dysfunctional little pearler when shopping in the sports section for hubby's latest distraction from your girthy tenant. He fossicks away near the squash racquets and you leave him to it.

Suddenly, you catch a scent that sends your senses into overdrive and stick your nose in the air to find the source. Up and down the aisles you waddle like a crazed bloodhound until you locate it. An open can of tennis balls and for whatever reason, you are drawn to them. Not in a freaky fetish kind of way, but in a freaky *must inhale* kind of way. You know.

Time seems to warp during this disturbing moment. It's not until Green Man shouts your name that you see two teens pointing and laughing at you breathing in the fluorescent, furry object with questionable glee. Nothing exists except you and these divine, hairy, green balls.

"What are you doing?" Green Man calls listlessly from afar.

"Ur, dunno. But I can't stop," you respond without removing the ball from your nostril. He slowly approaches, reaches down to the cannister and holds it towards you like he's luring a rabid dog about to maul a squirrel.

"I'll buy you a fresh tin if you will please stop whatever this is and come with me now."

"Okay," you reluctantly answer, placing the ball back on the shelf and leaving your giggling audience to mimic your madness. Excellent. You've graduated from ice-tray-lik-wid-choc-porky to ball-sniffing-weirdo. Could be worse.

On your way out you eye an extra-large bag of bullets and chuck them in the trolley. After your sudden sports goods enthusiasm Green Man nods approvingly, happy to encourage your more *normal* cravings. You wish he hadn't. His acceptance is a green light to gorge all the live-long-day and the influx of bingeing typically finds its way to your arse that is fast finding its way to triple butt proportions. Problem is you have so far to go in this pregnancy. But don't worry. Your frequent trips to the hospital are about to give those ham hocks a good old work out.

GO TO: PAGE 45

PAGE 7:
HE DOES!

(from page 48)

Hope you like canned beans and two minute noodles because that's all your broke arses will be eating for the next eighty years. At least until you pay this thing off.

One thing for sure – WOW! Mountain Buggy is one awesome pram and Green Man glows a little every time he walks past it. Multiple yays all-round, but to maintain this happy hubby vibe – maybe slow down the spending and let him recover a bit. The man is not incapable of building a wall across your vagina to prevent this baby from coming out and completely bleeding him dry.

Time to pull out the glitter pens and get cracking on the birth plan.

GO TO: PAGE 56

PAGE 8:
B) POSTPONE

(from page 1)

Green Man is a complicated cat. He's barely gotten over the whole wedding ordeal, so news that he is going to become a Father could tip him over the edge of the stability spectrum. You decide to wait. You're going to need all his wits on board for the main event.

You reason most people don't announce it to the world at least until *Week 12,* so that's what you'll do. He won't miss much. Just a couple of blood tests and checkups that he'd probably be bored shitless attending anyway.

You lament not being able to unleash the spare tyres and let the fun bags live a loose and free life. Never mind. You'll have to contain your lady lumps a little longer and cross your fingers morning sickness won't be too brutal.

GO TO: PAGE 76

PAGE 9:
TIME TO GO HOME

(from page 59)

Home time and your jaundiced little sunflower has had the all clear! Yay! Plus you've done something that resembles a poo and even if you hadn't you had no issue faking a shnarpo – anything to get out of here.

The Nurse is off getting the discharge papers, so you pack up your stuff and phone Green Man to come and collect his little family. As you look down at your beautiful bundle you are filled with love-fuelled elation. Sure he looks like a ninety-year-old goldfish with a dodgy tan, but he is radiating some heavenly vibes. You breathe in a big infant whiff and kiss his wrinkled little cheek. The pelvic scrape is healing nicely, and for the first time since you arrived on the ward, you feel a little less rattled. That is, until an unfamiliar midwife casually walks in. It's shift change again and you haven't seen this one before. Even more disconcerting – she is a stroller. The hairs on the back of your neck stand up. In your experience, no matter the industry – nothing good ever comes from strolling in the workplace. After your *midwitch* experience you feel a little uneasy about most people who walk through the door and your instincts soon prove worthy.

She looks in at bub and stares. And she stares some more. She stares way too much and you immediately panic. She knows nothing of your history and the nurse just took the papers with her. The hair pricking spreads to your arms alerting you to speak. You don't feel the need for your usual politeness, so something really is very wrong.

Cue *midwitch THE 2ND*.

"We're being discharged. I'm just waiting for the nurse to return with the papers."

"Mmm mm. What's this on baby's forehead?"

"A graze. He scraped himself on my pelvis on his way out."

"Doesn't look like a graze…"

"Well, it is and the nurses said it's healing nicely," you say then pause a moment. *What the hell else would it be?*

"Hmm. May need to be tested."

"Pardon?"

"Doesn't look right."

"The Nurse just told me it's healing. None of the doctors or anyone else has mentioned anything to the contrary. She's coming with the discharge papers now," you respond shakily. It's as if you know the next few moments will be another drama – and they are.

The Nurse with the papers floats in like an ethereal dream just in time, but when she sees *midwitch II* her airy mood dissipates.

"Oh. Are *you* on already? I didn't realise the time. Well, this beauty and her cutie are being discharged," she sweetly sings, and the relief overwhelms you. *Thank you floating paper holding angel!*

"Not until this is seen to. It's weeping," *midwitch II* responds with an air of authority.

FCk it! She outranks her!

"Oh? We've been monitoring it and it looked to be healing."

"It needs to be tested. Go and get *Dr Whoever*."

"Ur... well... they *are* being discharged."

"Go get him anyway," she responds in an eerie tone and you watch on as the angel nurse shrugs her shoulders and mouths,

"I'm really sorry" before exiting the room.

You are trying to keep it together, you really are. You take a deep breath and attempt to reason with *midwitch II*.

"I don't understand what's happening. Is my baby somehow infected? Is something airborne?" you ask. She ignores you and continues looking at bub. *Wrong answer lady.* "Excuse me. I just want to go home. Can you please tell me what's going on?"

"Precaution."

"A precaution for what?" you ask again as the nurse returns with an official looking person who is probably a doctor, but you no longer care. It's just another clueless someone who knows nothing of you or your bub. The doctor/official looking thing senses your angst and attempts some bedside manner.

"Hello there. I'm *Doctor Dunno*... we're juuusst going to have a little look at your young... ah... man here. Okay... mmm," he and *midwitch II* talk low. "Yep... ah yes, there *is* weeping..."

No effing shit! From the wound caused by my jagged pelvis! The wound that weeps because it's healing!

You feel like you're about to lose your mind. Hopefully Green Man will arrive soon to sort these prodders out. In a few hours you'll be laughing about it as you swaddle your babe close in the safety and comfort of your own bed. At home. Far away from here. You just need to breathe.

What will it be?

DO YOU:
A) A CHANGE OF PLANS: PAGE 58
B) LOSE YOUR BANANA: PAGE 39

PAGE 10: WRAP IT UP

(from page 64 & 84)

You end Green Man's torture. No point punishing him further and he *is* bringing the vibe down. You look at your reflection and touch your tum. It was never much of a flatty. This is going to be tricky to decipher what's baby and what's chunky. On the plus side you can stop walking around like a carrot with a hard-on pretending you don't have at least three tyres under that top. Come on now. That flowy shit is fooling no one. Embrace it!

You start ringing, posting, gramming, snapping, chatting, tocking and tweeting the news to half the planet's population. Everyone is thrilled and gifting you the normal reactions you've been denied by the one who helped create this situation.

You've been dreaming of having a baby since forever and contemplate the joy to come.

DO YOU:
A) START RESEARCHING: PAGE 21
B) SIT BACK AND RELAX: PAGE 78

PAGE 11:
B) HAIRY LITTLE OVERCOOKED WOMB LOVER

(from page 86)

The nursery has still not been painted. The girth continues to grow. The festive season fast approaches and you wish it would all just fa la la la la fark right off. Being preggo at this time of the year was not part of the plan. The one thing you really do not want is a Christmas baby. Everyone tells you how lovely it would be, but you're not buying the *it's not so bad having your birthday on Christmas day* spiel. Yeah right. It would suck and you've always felt sorry for people who do. Green Man's birthday is three days after the holy holiday and he fares just as bad as if it were the 25th. Everyone forgets. You forget. Your family forgets. His family forgets. His friends forget. Shit, even he forgets some years. He's like a leap year wizard baby. No one knows how old he is – not even him. You do not want your boy to suffer the same fate. But, as it nears ever closer, concern grows that your floaty foetus may be taking after you in the *I shall not pass the womb* department.

FLOATY BUTTERCREAM BABY BISCUIT FLASHBACK

Your parents tell a tale (half the planet has heard from their relentless over sharing) of baby swimming lessons down at the local bleach hole. While you worked a wedgied one piece like nobodies slippery, cellulited business – the entire class were fashionably forced against their will under water. On release, everyone made their traumatic way to the surface – spluttering and carrying on like infants betrayed. All protested except you. Having an elite athlete mother in her prime, it's likely she unknowingly thrust you a little further than the more gentle armed Mummies were capable of. No problem for chubba bubba! You unnaturally ascended to the surface like a floaty, buttercream biscuit giving a reluctant kick when the act of breathing threatened to keep you from your next meal. The entire swimming house stopped to watch the freakish phenomenon.

"Is she okay?" your mother asked the instructor and only person in the building not panicking at the sight.

"She's fine. She figured out she's naturally buoyant."

"Oh. Well that's good... I think?"

"Let me guess – she was overdue?"

"She was, actually."

"Water birth?"

"Good god no! Not a chance."

"Natural water-baby then. Impressive. She'll be a good swimmer, but probably too lazy to hone her skill."

"Well, that's... something to look forward to."

When you finally resurfaced like a slimy walrus calf, everyone gasped with relief. If they wanted speed, a juicy sea cucumber would have got things moving quicker. You loved it down there and the womby sensation of being underwater. You adored being in utero so much that your unwilling carcass had to be forcepped out, overcooked and resembling a hairy little alien.

"The exact words your Father used – 'She looks like a hairy little alien.'"

Charming.

Despite the disturbing flashbacks the tale seems rather precautionary. You rub your never-ending growing tum. There are many things you hope your child inherits from you, but being a buoyant-hairy-little-alien-womb-lover is not one of them.

That night you dream of the baby growing so big he sucks up all the fluid and takes over your body. You wake up in a cold sweat craving sea cucumbers. That nursery needs to be finished, though it's not looking promising.

GO TO: PAGE 37

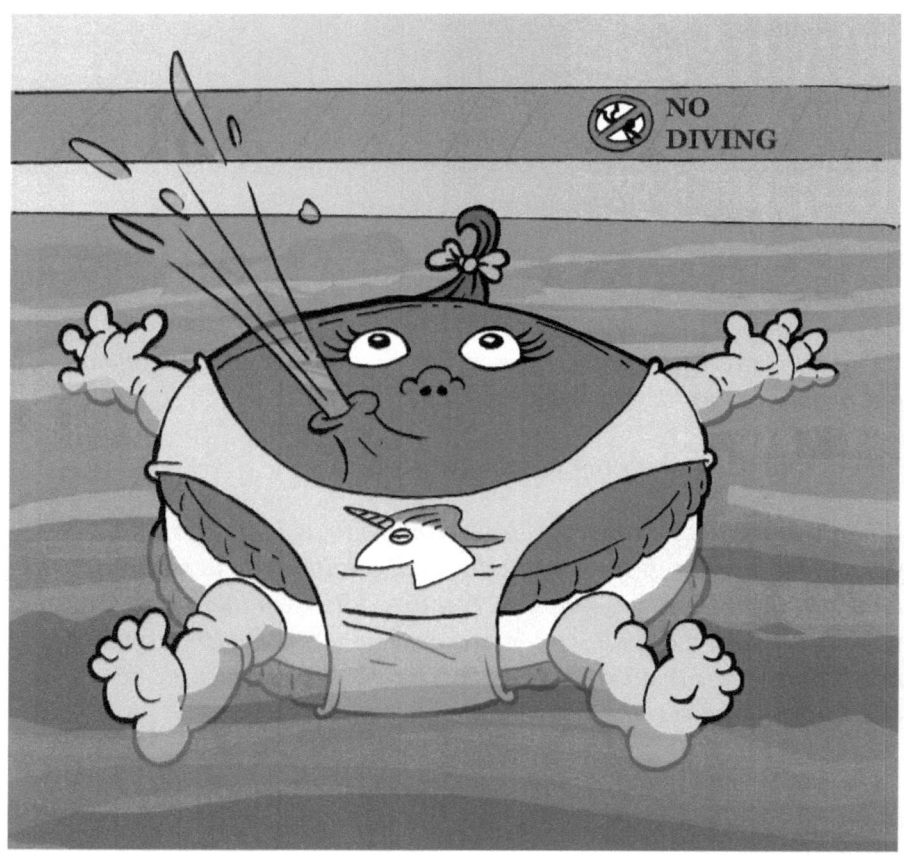

PAGE 12:
A) HEADS: C-SECTION

(from page 107)

That synchronised swimming has paid off and your little dipper has turned. No caesarean for you this time.

GO TO: PAGE 79

PAGE 13:
THE CAR BACK STORY

(from page 5)

CAR FLASH BACK

A week before you are due Green Man received his first ever company car. It was a big moment. A brand new car after years of knowing nothing but second-hand shit boxes was well deserved. Green Man is a proud man and has always extended that pride to the meticulous care and love shown to his possessions. One in particular was his former four-wheeled drive that he sacrificed in order to upgrade to a child appropriate automobile. Green Man's young man Pajero was an awesome vehicle rigged up with loads of off-road goodies. Like built-in drawers to hold bush-bashing shit, special feature thingies and custom made crap he and his mates would frequently toss over. It was his pride and joy and some great adventures were had during those blissful kid-free years in 'The Paj'. Unfortunately, to accommodate the quality crafted drawers the four seater had become a two seater.

GREEN MAN: How about I jimmy up an occy strap to the back door as a makeshift child harness?

YOU: Ur... probably no.

GREEN MAN: Why not?

YOU: *Well, it's not really gonna cut it with me, the law, or the world really.*

GREEN MAN: *Boo.*

So he very reluctantly sold his first baby to buy the family-friendly-funless-mobile with a psychotic amount of safety features included. He traded the epitome of youth and freedom – for a right royal baby buggering. He traded vintage blue – for powder blue. He traded unexplored possibilities – for sippy cup holders and built-in DVD's. He traded custom drawers – for his devil spawn to spend the majority of their childhood kicking the back of his seat over and over and over again. To add salt to the wounds the young guy he sold it to had just finished Uni and was off on his gap year around Australia. He looked uncannily like Green Man ten years prior. 'Twas quite the sucker punch.

You tried to excite him about all the fun adventures you would share as a family, but he was balls deep in Wallow Town to hear. Initially, you sympathise with his turmoil, but after nearly eight and a half months of listening to his woeful lamenting for metal and plastic – you were well and truly done. Boo bloody hoo. It's a car. He could get a new one. You, on the other hand, were probably not going to get an upgrade from the stretchy skin yard any time soon.

And so the flashback ends in fun-free flames of Green Man's reality.

RETURN TO: PAGE 46

PAGE 14:
BABY SHOWER

(from page 56)

You make the mistake of forgoing help from Bestie's family. She is due to have her bundle any day and you don't want to deprive her of her angel support team, just in case. Luckily your cousins are going to throw the most over the top extravaganza of a baby shower. You entrust them with your eighty six paged hand bound vision board spectacular, that you deliver to their workplaces in person and by the looks of their stagnant expressions they seemed not so super thrilled by your efforts.

Organising the baby shower has been an odd version of *fun* that filled the gaping void left by your former and frequent boozing. What is coming to fruition is how much *fun* you've been having particularly with online orders. The novelty packages arrive in droves. Teeny tiny baby bottles, giant dummies, nappies, games, prizes and enough decorations to throw a pastel themed wedding for seven hundred guests. The boxes keep coming so thick and fast you nearly run out of stash room. Luckily Green Man is oblivious, otherwise this could get a little tricky to explain. He has accepted most celebrations organised by you usually have a hefty after-party aftermath, but even you didn't realise how out of hand your late night shopping habits had become. You've been planning this shindig since you first found out the sex of the baby, and unbeknownst to the rarely bothered logical side of your brain, ole tappy fingers has been chip-chip-chipping away at the checkout trolley. Most are one-offs and will never be of use again – something you will find out ten years and three houses later when you discover them in all their unopened glory! Another problem for another decade.

For now, there is baby shower paraphernalia coming out the wazoo and you manage to store your hoard in a spare cupboard Green Man never opens. Phew. Now you just need your family of helpers to set it all up and weave their party planning magic. You look forward to their support. With every shove of every box of every passing day you are becoming slower, girthier and less coordinated than you already weren't.

Unfortunately, Cousin Lacey has taken ill and the baby shower committee are indisposed. On top of that, Green Man is away for work, family members who offered to help are all booked up and you feel like a prized dick asking Bestie for aid at the eleventh hour. If that wasn't enough, your doctor has recommended you take it easy – like some sad sack maiden from the fourteenth century. You're hefty, helpless and on your own. So like the toddler about to jump from a wobbly bedpost – you decide to go for it yourself, which will probably be on your top twenty list of dumbest moments ever.

The large amount of chores you've jotted down rolls onto the floor like the guest list to a jousting tournament. You ignore the echoes of *Hear ye! Hear ye!* and press on. Not even the town crier can help you now. You cart all the boxes out from their hiding places and soon the entire floor of your living room is covered. It's a big room and there is a lot of stuff. So. Much. Shit. There is no point moaning as you get to the task. You start at 10:30 that morning and finish just after midnight and the pain that was only present when you walked too far is now present when you walk two steps.

Oh dear. Watchya gonna do?

DO YOU:
A) CALL BESTIE: PAGE 81
B) SLEEP IT OFF: PAGE 63

PAGE 15:
B) GO OUT

(from page 75 & 88)

It's midweek and the outside world is alive in all their pre-holiday Christmas glow. *You all suck!!!* The internal screaming helps while you slurp on your first coffee in yonks. Might as well caffeinate it up seeing as there's no child to lap at your lattes right now. It tastes like shit, but takes immediate effect. You buzz about like a bee on steroids, crashing as quickly as you rose. Your body rudely reminds you of its primary duty and yay it's moo-moo time again. You make a mad dash to the lav's with gorged breasts and no baby to drink from them. You bless the lucky establishment with a little moo-moo show and watch the tainted, yet precious contents swirl down the dunny plughole. Au revoir.

You try to fix yourself up, but your efforts reflect nothing but a wrung out rubber glove. Green Man waits patiently at the pretentiously decorated table. He too is exhausted, but musters some concern.

"How was that?"

"Super."

"Are you okay?"

"Think I scarred a few yuppies, but I'll be fine.

"Will they be?"

"*They* could probably use a dose of maternal reality."

"Fair enough."

"Can we go back now? The test results may be in."

"Sure, but try not to get your hopes up. I don't want you to be upset."

"I'm beyond being upset."

"I know. Just try to keep it together."

Try to keep it together, or the act of keeping *it* together – will be suggested to you for many years to come by those who should probably worry more about their own *it* and less about yours.

You appreciate Green Man's concern and know he's trying to comfort you in a situation way beyond his emotional skill set.

Screaming might help – *OF COURSE I'M NOT KEEPING IT TOGETHER!* Thankfully, you don't, instead you grit down and pretend to keep on keeping *it* on.

Back at *Doomsville* the jolly staff have been decorating. Everyone is very pleased with their festive efforts and weird fifties deco, but you struggle to muster your usual polite enthusiasms. Yo fCking no.

All the babies have been swaddled in cute Christmas themed wraps and they each have tiny festive beanies. It's so beautiful that your spirits lift until you see your bub who is very festive-free. You rub his little bum and stare lovingly down at his sweet face and the tears stream again. While the prems look like bonny little holly wreaths, yours is bursting out of a plain onesie and a bright red beanie that barely reaches his ears. *S1* notices your deflation and offers some comfort.

"We found a red beanie that nearly fits. The Christmas wraps are too small, so we put one over his feet," she says and you look down at the festive foot warmer and it's nothing but twelve days of triggering all over again. The tears streak over what little makeup you put on in an effort to appear more in line with that previously mentioned *together* thing.

"Nothing fits him because he shouldn't be here," you blurt out in a lifeless monotone. You know it's a bratty response, but you're really struggling to contain the truth bombs now.

"He does look sweet though, Mrs Man. And look! We made something for you," she chirps and hands over a card with genuine joy. "It's your bubs tiny feet and his little handprints," she beams as you wipe the relentless tears that fall, smudging the bittersweet gift that never should have existed.

"Thank you. It's really sweet," you reply with honest gratitude.

"Baby's first bit of art," *S1* sings. She seems more pleased with her crafting skills than the actual sentiment, but you appreciate the effort regardless. She smiles and you soften a smidge toward her as she awkwardly scurries off to *S2* who dons her signature season look of indignance. Green Man puts his hand on your shoulder.

"He looks like a cherry about to burst," he says, softly.

"Yeah, he does. Our little plum pudding," you respond, manage a laugh and stretch the edges of the tiny beanie to stop it from squeezing his perfectly average sized, healthy infant head. You look at the troublemaking scar and curse your jagged pelvis for all the unnecessary bullshit it's caused. Green Man senses your brewing. After a few hours of no results he calls it a day and you both leave babyless again.

GO TO: PAGE 110

PAGE 16:
A) SLOW DOWN

(from page 82)

Nice one. Those baby hormones have lightened your vocal chords, filtering your angelic tones into his sense of logic and reason. He spends the rest of the evening getting tips on Fatherhood from your seven thousand relatives. You look at him lovingly and feel content. You all leave at a decent hour and head home. Green Man has a sensible nightcap, gets into bed and falls into a deep sleep.

You, however, are not tired and your back has begun to ache more than usual. A hot shower should do the trick. It does. You pull on your new maternity PJ's and lay your head on the pillow. A blissful feeling of peace washes over you and you fall into an Aurora-like sleep with dreams of being induced. Tomorrow is the day.

Let's get the real party started!

GO TO: PAGE 94

OR

IF YOU HAVE ALREADY GIVEN BIRTH TO BUMBALINA – TIME FOR SOME MISTER-MEANOUR

GO TO: PAGE 41

PAGE 17:
CRAVINGS AND HABITS

(from page 104)

If there is one thing your pre-baby self knew for certain – you would be destined to dive gob first into the delicious world of pregnancy cravings with untoned, wide-winged arms. Some women claim they never had cravings. You are not one of them and take up the challenge like you're a contestant on a bizarre food show. Salt and vinegar chip sandwiches become an incredibly unhealthy choice, thankfully shortly lived, though thoroughly savoured. You actually do eat everything you can and should to satiate a growing bub, but you also allow for indulgences of the most extreme.

Ice cream as a staple meal, jars of peanut butter and those stringy mozzarella cheese stick thingies make regular appearances on the menu. But, it's *Lik-Wid-Choc* that becomes the obscenely frequent feature – weekly, daily, then later on and disgracefully so, hourly. It starts off as dessert, an after dinner treat if you will, that turns into a late-night snack, that soon calls out from the pantry of an evening (yes the food talks too).

Eventually, you don't even bother with the ice cream element, cunningly ditching it and filling ice cube trays with the liquidy goodness and then gorging on what is essentially luscious chocolate blocks. Oh dear. You feel disgusted with yourself after every binge session for about seventeen seconds before you whip up another batch and unapologetically inhale that too.

You try to remedy your out of hand dessert sauce addiction by replacing it with liquorice bullets. It's criminal how many bags you manage to go through and poorly justify it as a digestive miracle-cure for your bunged up ailments. No one is fooled.

It gets way worse. One morning you look down to a rather unacceptable display of breakfast fare – a creative combo of strawberry sauce and *Lik-Wid-Choc* drizzled over a bed of ice cream... and lettuce. Deary, deary me. It seems little *Miss Irrationality* is implementing her squatter rights in what was formerly your brain and *'fCk it'* is the creed of the moment. You remind yourself to get that tattooed on your ankle after you've had the baby and forget it seven seconds later.

Ginger beer is still a firm favourite, until heartburn rears its hideous head and sticks around for the remainder of the pregnancy. Welcome to *antacid* world! Even though it tastes like regurgitated toothpaste and is a thousand times thicker – it works and you down it like water for that sweet release from the relentless discomfort now presenting itself when you consume air. It isn't until Green Man walks in on a mid-morning pang-fest that things turn around. A bit.

GM: Why are you awake? Is everything o... kay... wait. What are you doing now?

YOU: Eating.

GM: You're sculling *Lik-Wid-Choc* straight from the bottle.

YOU: I'm fine. Go back to bed.

GM: This does not look fine. It's disturbing.

YOU: She's all good mate.

GM: Are you an ocker now?

YOU: If it makes you bugger off and leave me to gorge in peace, too bloody right, cobber.

Thankfully, Green Man recognises the psychotic sugar spiral you've wound yourself into and makes it his mission to provide green smoothies and the occasional bit of protein. Your nostrils are still very anti-meat, but your body ignores them as you devour every last morsel before the onset of diabetes. Things ease up eventually and you soon discover an appealing smell for the first time during the pregnancy.

But, before that violation against all things rational – it's time for Antenatal classes!

Onya bike!

GO TO: PAGE 95

PAGE 18:
A) A DAY OUT

(from page 86)

In the city. Completely sensible and just what you need. A touch of window shopping, maybe pick up some last-minute onesies to throw on the pile and a light lunch. Bahahahaha! Who are you kidding? A seven-course degustation set menu with optional extras where cannibalism isn't out of the question. Bring it.

You do need to buy a dress for what is apparently the year of the wedding, so you could kill a few birds and BBQ them… or something about a stone metaphor. Mercy. Things really are melting. The biggest melter of them all is that you fail to take into account that it is Christmas. 'Tis the season **not** to take a pregnant body downtown. Thousands of people. Much overheating. Many melting moments and not the edible kind. Overcrowded situations and violations of personal space of which you take up a lot of.

And then there is that fun, excruciating, sharp-shooting pain occurring in the pelvic region the further you walk. At first you feel okay, but then every step becomes unbearable. Balls. Now you can't even shop? Turd burger baby clearly disagrees with this method of filling your time and is already showing signs of his Father's lineage of irritation when shopping.

So much for your respite efforts. You are so over the bedridden thing, but it looks like you have little choice other than taking it easy for the remaining days.

Perhaps some lighter, less ambitious options?

DO YOU:
A) AQUA AEROBICS: PAGE 83
B) WALK THE DOG: PAGE 25

PAGE 19:
A) FALL INTO A HEAP

(from page 38)

This shit is too over the top and the smelly lot hits you hard. You're not much of a delicate collapser, more of a slumper and you kind of melt onto the ground and just lay there quietly palpitating, eye twitching. At least you know the floor has been heavily disinfected. People have gathered and Green Man is slapping you gently on the cheek. They all seem a million miles away. You feel like you are floating. *Was that a needle prick?* Probably. Sedation would be an all-time anticlimactic low.

Somehow you make your way to the car and wake up the next morning in a pool of your own milk. Dreams of white coats and floating babies make you shiver, though it's actually the saturated sheets. They stink and so do you. You have a shower, wash the hideousness away and go into some sort of psychotic stealth mode where all that matters is bringing your misdiagnosed baby home.

Oh… and the spaceships are back.

Maybe kick this plan into gear once you wake up.

GO TO: PAGE 72

PAGE 20:
A) TAKE GREEN MAN

(from page 33)

Congrats! It's a set of nuts! You're having a boy! And a family first. You hail from a bloodline of nothing but firstborn fanny birthers. Fanny, after fanny, after fanny. You were the first born, as was your mother, as was her mother, as was hers and there's an enthusiastic Aunty somewhere with way too much time on her hands who has traced the family lineage for aeons. She claims the fannying goes way back.

Regardless, it is made abundantly clear from the day you get your period – that tradition-carrying-womb of yours better be packing nothing but ovaries, lest you disappoint a bunch of ghosts. An unbroken chain for… let's just say many generations, until now. You feel a pang of guilt for a millisecond and then smile, oddly. A record-breaking boy. Hee hee, hell yeah. Dad reckons it's because of a navy scoober diving stint, but you're not buying his underwater sperm issues. The reason is obvious – anti-conformity right down to your coding. THAT is super cool.

You wonder what the hell you would do with a girl anyway. You've been put off by the prospect of your own little pinky-pie thanks to your Mother who has been telling you since you were sixteen that one day your daughter would do all the same shitty, crazy crap to *you*. You smile even wider and *HA-HA* like a super-villain. *Sorry Mum, not today! It's teeny weeny little testosterone filled nurries all the way for this chicky!* You tap your fingers and grin manically. You and your son have cracked the curse and surely only good can come from gloating about it.

While you do something resembling the pregnant running man, Green Man has turned a somewhat perplexed shade of pickle.

"What's up? Want a refund?" you poke.

"Ur..."

"Hey, are you okay? Aren't you excited? You're going to have a son!"

"Yeah, yeah... wow... a little boy..."

Your cocking eyebrow tingles and you suspect there is more to Green Man's usual less-than-conventional response to yet another of life's beautiful moments.

"It's all good babe. You're gonna be a great Dad."

"I don't know if I'll know how."

"Ay? Why not? You'll be mint," you say and hug him. He offers a small smile and you feel for him, for not checking in with how he is fairing amongst all this newfound baby madness. You snuggle in later that night and the two of you briefly reconnect in a much needed, sweet moment. Alas, it all comes to an abrupt halt when he releases a fart that's been trapped in some foul stench pocket of his bowels since the eighties and that's the end of that. Let it never be said you did not try to service his feelings. Sabotaged by toxic fumes. Typical.

Enough of fluffy Mcpuffbutt and his violent windy pops. You need to seek the company of some tightly puckered arse lips of the feminine variety.

You and Bestie are off to a Baby Convention. Good luck with that.

GO TO: PAGE 68

PAGE 21:
A) IMMEDIATELY STARTS RESEARCHING

(from page 10, 57, 71 & 78)

You begin researching every hospital in the country and the road is not as simple as you initially thought it would be. Choosing is tricky. It seems everyone has their opinions, which you quickly learn people freely give even when you don't ask for them. Funnily this will continue long after the baby is born and apparently never seems to end. Enjoy that. You consider getting a plate made so you don't grind your teeth down to nubs, or gnaw your tongue off which you will frequently want to do from the inundation of other's well-meaningness. Enjoy that too.

For now, this is your moment and though it's scary as hell you are super excited about finally being one of those women who are actually in control of what happens to them. Yay, good for you. Cherish that fairy tale for these few seconds before it becomes abundantly clear that little ole you will have but a beetle's dick worth of say in your baby journey. But, you do have a choice in the location of where you will eventually have minimal choice. Confused and slightly horrified? Grab your shit rowing paddles and climb aboard.

What's it to be baby Mumma? A la natural? Or minimal pain land?

DO YOU CHOOSE:

A) PRIMAL WOMBING HOUSE FOR YOUR WHOLE FAMILY: PAGE 106
B) PRIVATE HOSPITAL FOR YOU & YOUR PRIVATES: PAGE 47

PAGE 22:
THE PARTY

(from page 25 & 31)

Belonging to a big family means next level get-togethers, and boy do they throw 'em big. You've always found it comforting being related to most people in the room. You could be standing next to a stranger at a funeral, when suddenly an Aunt drops an "Oh, you lot are cousins" and boom – instant connection. And this family is a goodie to be a part of, where years can pass and it will feel like you only saw them yesterday. Easy going and open to a gathering for any occasion, always accompanied by an overindulgence of food, booze and good times.

For some reason you always get butterflies just before arriving at these big shin-digs, but today they aren't there at all – which should have been a blazing warning sign of things to come. For now, all you feel is calm and grateful to be surrounded by your stellar kin.

You give the birthday man a big kiss as he pats your belly and makes his sweet, silly jokes. He is a staple of happiness in your memory bank, always laughing and joyous with an endless charity for all. At sixty is still the coolest cat. You adore him.

You are shuffled from relative to relative who collectively gush over the protrusion coming from your midriff. You finally make your way to the good seats where the rickety relatives and their ailing bodies gather in beautiful spirits. You love it here between the safety and comfort of Nan and Aunties, your go-to since you were a little girl.

One Aunty has upgraded her chair with a set of wheels and loads of special features. Her eyes light up when she sees your girth and summons you over. You rest your arm on the soft wool pads and hold her hand. It's like home.

"You know this is the best spot next to your favourite Aunty. They all come to you here," she whispers, squeezing your hand with what control she still has and manages to give you a wink. She's been whispering insider information to you your entire life and you adore her cheeky wit. She occupies her own special memory pocket in your mind. One where the sounds of Super Trouper[1] and Chiquitita[2] are on repeat and she forever struts through the haze in patent pink stilettos – channelling Anni-Frid and Pat Benatar with her glorious mane of tizzied hair. The embodiment of glamour and rock and most fitting at your sixth birthday – a KISS themed one. She was like a celebrity and you'll never forget that beautiful era when your Aunty was larger than life and still mobile within it.

She motions for you to lean closer.

"You're going to have that baby on Christmas day," she whispers, poking your huge rotund belly.

"I am bloody not."

"You are. I know these things. I can feel it."

"No way! He's already overdue and I don't want a Christmas baby."

"I'm sorry, but that's what he's going to be. You know I'm never wrong," she confidently states, smiling wickedly. "Except I was wrong about you having a boy. I'm still not happy about that."

---

[1] *Super Trouper: Benny Andersson and Björn Ulvaeus*

[2] *Chiquitita: Benny Andersson and Björn Ulvaeus.*

"Can't change that now Aunty," you giggle.

"You broke the chain."

"What chain?" you ask, knowing full well what she refers to.

"The first-born girls."

"Ah, that chain. I've always been different."

"You're exactly like your Mum. You're a good one. He'll be a good one too… but…"

"But what?"

"You still owe me a girl."

"No worries. I'll pop this one out and get straight on it shall I?"

"Yes please."

A few years later you grant her wish and present your little Bumbalina. She is one of the few people that approves of the name choice (probably because everyone else is so anti it) and you can't love her enough for moving to the beat of her own drum, always in defence of yours. Her eyes beam when you bring her to visit.

But, as time wears on, so does your Aunt's weary body and she is soon forced to hold court from her bedroom. When she knows you and Missy are coming she demands her minions stock the cupboards with lollies and sweeties and then delights at the hyperactive effects they have on her great-great niece. She manages to smile and watches on as the girl she'd requested commando rolls across the bed and over the limp limbs your Aunty no longer governs.

When her speech becomes harder to understand and your life becomes busier, the visits become less. You drive past her house most days with the intention of dropping in, but other distractions take priority. "Next week Aunty" you subliminally promise her, until one day there are no more next weeks. When she is gone you are consumed with a heavy sorrow that the Aunty who always saw the good in you, who gave and gave and gave to you and so many who were lucky to know her, was gone forever. You never said goodbye. You never said thank you. You never told her how much you loved her. You are never rid of a guilt that you abandoned her when she became too difficult to understand. When it was too sad for you to expose yourself to her slow and suffering demise. When you used the madness of life as an excuse. When a visit from you and your crazy kids is all she would've needed to feel like she was still loved, wanted and useful. You will forever regret not reflecting her light when she needed it most.

#multiplesclerosisfuckingsucks

But that is for a sad, sad time far, far away.

Right now, the party is getting lively and the liquor is flowing. Your cousin is up to mischief. A mischief that will have you cursing him and your wicked family for the next decade to come.

GO TO: PAGE 82

PAGE 23:
BEDRIDDEN

(from page 42)

Well. This. Is. Balls. They might as well prescribe hot towels and leeches, because being bedridden seems way too distressed-damsel and you're having none of it. You feel fine.

To make things worse, this is proving to be the most season defying weather ever known in the history of the earth. The sun just shines on like the show-casing arsehole it is and all day long you hear horrible, happy humans living their best outdoor lives and you hate every single one of them. You consider jimmying up a little slingshot so you can ditch olive pips at ecstatic out-and-abouters, lord knows you've got a hefty source of salty ammunition from your new found craving. You decide against it, draw the blinds and channel your inner mushroom.

Whilst you have physically admitted defeat, there is absolutely nothing wrong with your tongue of which you now lash out your disdain to the walls on an hourly basis. Poor Green Man has decided to work from home to keep an eye on you. That sympathy train rapidly derails when he grasps the full extent of your frustrations and chugs back to the safe zone of the industrial wastelands. As far as patients go – you're just a dick.

What was once a teenage dream to laze around like a stoned lummox, watching TV and pigging out all day – has become the stuff of nightmares. You've got shit to do and nothing has been done. There's a nursery to sort, baby clothes to be bought and a hospital bag to be packed. All put annoyingly on hold while you've taken up knitting, egg shell art, birdwatching, plane spotting, scrap booking and an unhealthy obsession for the lifestyle channel that has you drawing up plans for a second story extension, and a tiny home that attaches to the bike you don't own.

You vent your shit in Haiku form.

WHICH ONE:

A) CALM: PAGE 111

So much still to do

Season sun doth warm my son

I shall wait it out

OR

B) A LESS RATIONAL APPROACH: PAGE 92

So much crap to do

Bedridden has knobs on it

Sun can fCk right off

PAGE 24:
THE MIDWITCH

(from page 87 & 112)

This woman does not go away. She's one monocle and an eerie whistle off a super villain and you swear she's got it in for you. Like, what the shit? It had been three days since you last saw her and you thought you'd dodged a bullet. She recognises you immediately and smells your fear. She may, or may not have sharp teeth when she smirks, but that could also be a little tittie pressure hallucination.

There's no escaping it. *midwitch* is your only salvation.

She leers like a piranha. You already know she has zilch bedside manner and now you get to discover how rough she is too. The *midwitch* is testing every method in her outdated breastfeeding bag of tricks, whether or not you want to be tested on. Bub sleeps soundly, which apparently is irrelevant as she yanks him up and launches him at your chest. Nothing has even happened yet and just holding bub against you hurts like hell. You know eventually you will have to nourish your newborn and you can't walk the earth with screaming melons forever.

FUTURE SCREAMING MELONS BRA SHOPPING HALLUCINATION:

"What size bra are we looking for your howlers today?"

"Just give me those umbrellas."

"That's part of our winter display, dear."

"Get out the gaffer tape and strap 'em on, lady. I ain't playin."

The angel Midwife had briefly shown you some latching techniques and positions, but at no point was she forceful with you or bub. You wish she was here. You don't mind bossy women, but the vibe from the *midwitch* is cold and cantankerous. Nothing about this feels right.

She pulls your gown back and motions for you to whip out the tit. There's no need for whipping – they're like erect globes awaiting invasion. She tweaks the obscenely swollen nipple so hard it feels like needle piercing. *midwitch* takes her whole hand behind your precious bubba's head, then thrusts both tiny infant mouth and Mother's breast in an abrupt, aggressive act. Little sharky begins his head turning routine, but she's having none of it. Holding his entire head tightly forward, the *midwitch* forces him to engulf your scorching areolas. His little eyes open wide and you see a panic that no one should ever see in a three-day-old. Your baby is scared. He attempts to cry, but she continues to push him against your searing pain. He tries turning his head frantically from side to side, but again she repositions him in the name of *optimum flow* that now spurts over his face and eyes and is distressing him even more. Blobby tears roll down your sweet baby's cheeks as you both make eye contact. You take his reaction as one of two possible things:

He is pleading for your help to make it stop.

OR

He thinks *you* are causing his dismay.

A surge of manic flows through you. Despair, sorrow, confusion, hatred, betrayal. Most Mothers are ready to experience strong emotions days after giving birth, but surely nothing this extreme and most definitely not during a breastfeeding session. It comes bitterly thick and you cannot talk yourself out of despising this wretched witch with her shunting hands of doom probing and prodding your son and your body without once asking if any of it is okay.

Mini-Man's breathing becomes more frantic as he attempts to find air through his tiny little nostrils that are still being shoved against your smothering skin. The ordeal is stressing him into a panicked state. He is choking. This crock of insanity plays out in a matter of seconds. The entire time you look from your child, to this bitterly determined hag and somewhere in the background you know it is all causing you an excruciating amount of pain.

You have read a tonne of reassuring books and pamphlets and been told by countless Nurses, Midwives, Doctors and fellow Mums that breastfeeding sessions are always facilitated by kind, reassuring Midwives trained in creating safe, warm and nurturing spaces for both Mother and infant. But this experience is a dark, dark reflection. It feels like she is on her own point-proving mission and you and your son *will* be tamed.

You are *not* being over the top.

You are *not* being a drama queen.

You are *not* hallucinating.

This is really happening and it is getting out of hand.

DO YOU:
A) DEMAND SHE CEASE! PAGE 3
B) RECLAIM YOUR BREASTS! PAGE 26

PAGE 25:
B) WALKING THE DOG

(from page 18)

Get some fresh air and take the dog for a walk, all the normal non-pregnant people with normal non-hyperactive dogs say. Just putting a lead on your jittery pooch is like trying to put a slippery doughnut over a snappy sea lion. You finally manage it and you, pup and your heaviness head out to the driveway. Two steps in and you nearly pass out. Holy moly you have whacked it on and when did legs become such a bitch to navigate? You've taken eight steps and you're panting!

While you plead with your respiratory system not to pack it in, the dog decides he is going to relieve his bladder of what appears to be three hundred years' worth of puppy piss. It's exhausting to watch and just as you are about to venture onto the road – it's snapper time. At least he had the decency to crap on your turf rather than the verge warrior's pristine lawn of the *best-kept street in the worst-kept suburb.* You go to get a poo bag and remember that level of preparation would have involved an organised state of mind, one you've not housed for many moons. You look at your dog. He looks at you. You both look at the steaming turd. You swear he says *"Sod it"* and that's all you need to turn your weary and hallucinating butt back inside. Luckily Green Man pulls up just in time to pooper scoop and burn some energy off your poor neglected fur baby. He grabs the lead and raises a brow.

"Walking the dog? Really?"

"Just came back, actually. Feeling fantastic."

"Mmm mm," he responds with an all bullshit-knowing smirk smothering his face. You shrug up a *meh* storm and waddle inside guilt-free. Puppy distracts him by pulling at the lead until Green Man is forced to follow. You know a sea lion who'll be getting extra snappy snacks tonight.

Hey, you gave the whole movement thing a semi-go. Go rest up for the party of the century.

GO TO: PAGE 22

PAGE 26:
B) RECLAIM YOUR BREASTS

(from page 24)

Indeed, you do. You manipulate your mammaries out of her spindly fingers of witchiness and take matters into your own clueless hands. Suddenly your milk is well and truly *in* and arrives with such force it flows like a hydrant. It does not stop!

GO FOR IT MILKY TITS!

The *midwitch* is gasping for air and dog paddles through the breasty flood. You fill the room with your pristine milk-making magnificence! All you need are some oats and the entire hospital could have a hearty feed of porridge! How very *Brothers Grimm*.

Or…

This could be yet another hallucination brought on by the severity of your boobie blockages.

Of course it is.

Come back to reality Goldilocks. There could be some bear hugs and a bowl of porridge in it.

GO TO: PAGE 3

PAGE 27:
A) THE FOOD HALL

(from page 68)

If you thought the stalls section was bad, this scene is even worse. Hungry women are one thing. Hungry, exhausted, irritable pregnant women en masse are something to run far the fCk away from.

Disgruntled husbands line up like soldiers on a swat mission. They nervously focus on not muffing up the order while the wrathful vessels carrying their unborn children send subliminal threats from afar. It's a cold, cold war. To make matters worse, every second woman waddling to the line looks ready to burst and all are hangry as hell. These brave and chivalrous men sacrifice their spots to death glaring females, who with their pregnancy prowess, bully them into submission. All options are damned. Piss off a pregnant stranger, or throw themselves on the bollocking bomb of their insatiable partner?

March on to your inevitable fates brave warriors! Every choice is doomed!

Even with a tray brimful of food something will be wrong, or forgotten and the skulking wheel of skulking men, supporting their swollen viper women spins on. You can't help but feel sorry for them for about 3.7 seconds.

You and Bestie watch on wide-eyed. You are both hungry and incredibly thirsty, but there is no way you are entering that violation of sanity for a bucket of cold, crusty chips and a lukewarm cuppa that will cost you $49.89 and that's the *eXpo special!* The two of you link arms and stagger towards the exit. Drive through Maccas it is. #notummyleftbehind

DRIVE THRU CHICK: Welcome to McDonalds, just order when you're ready.

YOU: Ummm... I'd like a flame-grilled burger, please.

DRIVE THROUGH CHICK: This isn't HJs, Ma'am. And *all* their burgers are flame grilled. You can't just order a *flame grilled burger*.

YOU: I'll order whatever I want whipper snapper. Forget it!

Bestie cries tears of hilarity at your ludicrous outburst and even more when your clap back exit hits a snag. There are three cars in front of yours. You can't broggy your way out of this one. Not only are you blocked in, but the DTC stares at you with a bored glaze of belligerence. You are just another moron on a long list of morons she will have to deal with for the next eighteen hours on minimum wage. You remember being that girl. Serving the general public highlighted some valuable life lessons in the management of one's moral compass. None shined brighter than *all-you-can-eat-for-fCk-all* nights when every rock on the planet seemed to be lifted and all the scabs came out to play. Overloading plates just because they could, leaving untouched food scattered across trashed tables and still having the gall to demand extra discounts. Or sending half-eaten food back for a full refund because little Johnny *didn't really like it*. Having a teenage tongue-sword dripping with whip-lashing sarcasm was not your greatest asset in the food & beverage industry. A few patrons learned their own lessons in not pissing off the people who prepared the food. You can only imagine the bullshit fast-food staff deal with these days, but are too hungry right now for empathy. But good news! While you daydreamed about arseholes of long ago – Bestie hobbled next door and ordered a bagful of flame-grilled goodies for you both. Nom nom nom. Thirty five minutes later you leave the non-HJs drive-thru slightly embarrassed, yet satisfied. You whisper "sorry" as you drive by. DTC nods forgivingly, probably foreseeing her own future staring back at her.

This baby growing business is creating tension on the denim. Time for some shopping.

GO TO: PAGE 93

PAGE 28:
A) WAG IT

(from page 45)

Seriously? Are you sixteen? You're having a baby not sneaking off for a duzza behind the outdoor ed shed. Get your rebellious arse outta here!

GO TO: PAGE 35

PAGE 29:
CANDLE LIT DINNER

(from page 73)

It's dinner date night where partners come in and the staff offer to take bub for a bit so you can enjoy a battery operated candlelit dinner for two. Why there is a need to be romantic three days after giving birth with no chance of a happy ending for anyone – is a mystery. But you've heard how lovely this is for other couples and have been looking forward to it in the lead-up. The lead-up that involved a full night's sleep.

As with most nights here, the clang of bedpans and sounds of women in pain make for interesting mood music. Throw into the mix your still very exhausted state particularly after this morning's *SUPERDICK* eye-opener – it's no surprise you are reluctant to spend five minutes with anyone, let alone your husband. So, what is supposed to be a sweet, relaxing experience turns into an argumentative shit-show that includes overcooked steak and you bursting into hysterics every ten seconds.

"You look knackered," Green Man casually remarks and scrunches his face. Oh dear. The fool doth not knoweth what he hath unleashed-eth.

"Oh really? How am I supposed to look when I gave birth three days ago and had about twenty eight minutes sleep since?"

"Holy shit, babe. Calm down. I just meant you look really tired!"

"Of course I'm fCking tired! When I fall asleep the baby wants to eat. When she sleeps everyone seems to be inside my eardrum!"

You are not at your charming best right now. Green Man has unknowingly walked into a hostile, terrorist type situation he was not properly briefed on. In your defence and given your obvious state – you just want someone to read between your twitchy, unhinged lines. How hard is it to get the green light to lose your shit for really ridiculous reasons and not be questioned? Apparently quite hard when you're behaving like an unstable yeti.

Green Man calls it a night and returns in the morning with flowers in the hope he can lure out one of your nicer personalities. You accept them graciously and give him a hug. He looks at you like he is waiting for something in return. You raise an eyebrow. He dares suggest remorse.

"Is there anything you'd like to say to me?"

"Sure. She who has just given birth and only had a few hours' sleep in nearly four days shall apologise for shit-all," you spout like it's an ancient saying, from an ancient culture that sensibly worshipped ancient preggos and knew better than to bring stupid ancient expectations to their exhausted, ancient presence. Thankfully, Green Man lets it go as a Nurse pops her head in and asks if you are ready to go home. You pack up immediately even though they offer you a few more days.

"Hell no, thank you!" is your erratically polite response. It seems a lot of the other parents have the same idea as you filter out with familiar faces all panda-eyed and mumbling. You walk past the waiting room and there is *SUPERDICK* throwing his hands in the air. The munted Mummy, who looks like she's finally had an intravenous coffee, rips into him. He looks deflated and walks to the door. He seems to recognise you and freezes. You can't help but glare at him sternly and he scurries back to his partner.

"Get back in there and take it!" You want to yell, but thankfully don't. You never see them again, but over the years will come across many versions of *SUPERDICK* to make you cringe. Fortunately, they are outnumbered by many gorgeous, awesome Fathers having a stellar crack and just getting on with it like the rest of us.

It gives you hope for your little lass and her future as a woman of the world. Not that you have too much to worry about. This one comes out like an irritated babushka, behaving like she's lived a few lives on earth before. She most likely ruled empires – not as a queen – but an Empress. Empress Non-fCkery.

You notice she too has a hairy eyeball aimed at *SUPERDICK* and you swear a tiny voice says *"Bow down peasant."* Clearly you need sleep as bub may or may not have thrown you a regal wink before settling back into your arms.

When you make it home you and Bumbalina tuck into bed and finally rest, though your boobs soon let you know that full nights of slumber are a thing of the past. After the hospital stay you're grateful for even two hours of solid sleep in a row. Green Man is also grateful for the nicer version you become when you get those two hours and encourages the plight of sleep in the first crucial months of becoming parents.

The world thankfully continues to spin.

The End

If you would like to slum it a bit and experience a whole other level of complete madness –

GO BACK: PAGE 104

PAGE 30: GREEN MAN GIVES MAN-CHILD A BATH

(from page 97)

There is nothing cooler than a man in love with his child and that's what Green Man is. He strokes his son's hair and kisses his warm skin and breathes in his heavenly scent that is becoming less angelic with every passing day the little stinker goes without a wash. One of the Midwives is due to come and give Green Man a lesson on baby bathing, which is lucky because you've secretly been giving bub the once over and you're running out of wipes. You've been told to let his natural oils do their thing, but you still have your pregnancy **Super Smell** and baby's 'natural oils' are bringing tears to your eyes and not maternally.

It is pretty awesome that partners are encouraged to give bub their first bath and feel included in the whole new baby experience. It must be full on for the non-birthers to suddenly have this tiny little dependent and what was formerly their partner before them like a dried out sponge. Green Man takes to the duty with an impressive enthusiasm. Mini-Man takes to water like he was born in it. Kicking and flailing in protest of his exposed bits, Mini-Man soon melts into the warmth, creepy lizard eyes widen and his soggy little body goes all limp and floaty. Green Man lathers him up and the bath bonding begins with such tenderness and efficiency. You feel a wave of pride. He will be a great Dad and is a supreme network of support in the coming months when you are finding your way. Well done on your procreation choice. You forgive his sloppy efforts of the birth night, though you never, ever, ever forget. Mwa. Ha. Ha.

GO TO: PAGE 55

PAGE 31: WEDDINGS, PARTIES, BIRTHS

(from page 62 & 83)

Not a damn invitation to any event for nearly two years when you were hopping around a champagne guzzling-flat-stomached-avid meat-eater. Now every second person you know is getting married, or having a milestone birthday you can't get out of. The plot continues as sushi platters and anti-fricken-pasto are all anybody wants to serve and it's clearly a conspiracy you will complain to someone about. You forget it sixteen seconds later and randomly find yourself standing in front of the fridge humming Irish mourning tunes to a plate of leftover chicken. Just another meat you can't eat. Boo.

Bloody hen's nights, kitchen teas, fortieths, fiftieths, weddings and every hurrah in between are happening this year. The last wedding you were carrying nicely and managed to pull off a dress like a preggo goddess. It was a 'moment' and paired perfectly with some bathroom hilarity that would be one of the funniest sober nights you've ever experienced.

DRUNKEN BESTIE'S DRUNKEN BOOBIES FLASHBACK:

In a gorgeous scarlet fifties frock you stood guard at the bathroom door redirecting guests to an alternative ladies' room. Bestie was recently belly-free and quickly got the hang of things in the breast department with some itty-bitty-titty breathalising booze tabs. A very – "this baby shall not change my partying" – kind of way. Her beautiful baby girl was home with her angel Mum and Bestie had strategically squeezed out a healthy supply of BM ready to go. But, she misjudged the timing and her expressing enthusiasm sparked an onslaught of supply. You both indiscreetly smuggled her watermelons into the lav's with much leakage and giggling. Squeezing breast milk down the toilet felt a little uncouth and you suggested she milk-away straight into the sink. She beat you to it. There is nothing more comical than finely dressed women and wayward squirting boobs at a well-to-do event. Empty tits, half a champagne and a nip of vodka later, Bestie emerged as planet Par-Tay – heartily requesting Spice Girls and a pole. Having a baby can do funny things to reserved women. She busted out her side-shoe shuffle repertoire with extra oomph as wedding guests eagerly gathered round applauding her spectacular spectacle of freedom after nine months of baby making. Though you had a while to go, Bestie's show was inspiring. It made you keen to whet your own whistle and get yo boogie on.

You cack yourself at the memories that feel so long ago and lament over your current predicament. You've barely survived wedding season and there is one shindig to go. One of your favourite Uncles is having a big 60th and you are well overdue. This wouldn't be such a big deal to get out of if you weren't related to half the country who are invited. Everyone will be there. Which means no matter your situation – so will you.

You shelve the *Lik-Wid-Choc* and lay out your clothing choices on the bed. It's grim. You narrow it down to muumuu, eighties sack, tent wear, or a flesh revealing, stretchy frock made from synthetic materials that will most definitely result in chemical burns and ta-ta's to your cha-cha's. Bestie loans you a maxi dress she donned in the final months of her pregnancy. It's perfect and it fits.

Last legs of the third trimester and hopefully the last party. Better give rent-a-crane a call. It's time to come down from the tower and be sociable, Rapunzel.

Off to your Uncle's you go…

GO TO: PAGE 22

PAGE 32:

PART 2
THE MIDDLE

PAGE 33: WELCOME TO THE MIDDLE

(from page 32)

The fun times of the second trimester. You're in much better spirits and enjoying every second of the pregnancy. Bumpy has finally presented and you convince yourself that the skinny jeans still fit.

Green Man soldiers on and after the *Amnio* episode the severity of having a baby seems to sink in. He finally comes around with frequent hugs and sweet words. You bond, birds chirp, the sun shines and all is one with the world for the briefest of moments. But things slowly return to what shred of normality the two of you never really had. The routine of work, life and preparing for the big moment kicks back in along with the anxiety of becoming a Father. While you blanket yourself in all things maternity – Green Man copes by volunteering for the sudden influx of unusually frequent work trips. Conferences, seminars and schmooze events he previously could not have given a shit about, are randomly on the agenda and he welcomes any distraction from the increasing baby madness. While his work colleagues laugh at his inability to accept the inevitable, Green Man soldiers on in the insane hope that the whole ordeal may not happen. Like there could actually be a chance it will magically go away. Not in a bad sense. More like a time machine may appear and turn back the clock for him to whip a sneaky condom on mid-baby shag to prevent his current reality. Yes. This is the space Green Man resides in.

You briefly question your own poor choice of a procreation partner and ignore this unnecessary waste of your body's energy – better served forming ear lobes, or contemplating cake for breakfast. You leave him to it and immerse yourself into the exciting world of being an expectant Mum! It's definitely time to celebrate the coming of this baby and have some fun. Lucky for you baby is barely a bumpy and you're not at the banquet-feast-for-one stage just yet, so mobility is still a happening state. What better time to rejoice than finding out the sex of bub!

Who you gonna go with?

DO YOU CHOOSE:
A) GREEN MAN: PAGE 20
B) BESTIE: PAGE 65

PAGE 34:
VISITING HOUR FROM HELL

(from page 3)

Of all the visitors that could have come at this moment! Your bosses? Really? Exactly how many mirrors did you break as a child? If only they had walked in minutes before they could have seen the reasons behind the less than picturesque scene before them. One boss is visibly in shock and pretty much remains that way until she leaves. She later confesses she felt pity and simply didn't know how to react to a state she had rarely seen you in – a vulnerable and traumatised one. You can't blame her. You really are a red hot mess.

The other boss is a former Midwife who flits in like the Maternity Fairy sprinkling pixie dust all over your shitshow and going into the most impressive damage control ever. As you try to explain the situation she relieves you of bub and cuddles him close. He settles quickly, soothed by the definition of what a nurturing Midwife actually is. She puts him back into his incubator, rolls it over to the window, opens the huge dusty blinds like they do in old movies and the light blazes in.

"Let's give this beautiful boy some sunshine! Look Mister! Nature has all you need," she sings as the sunlight streams in and her blonde hair shines so brightly it looks like a halo.

You watch on like a bedraggled cup of noodles. Your hair is matted. Your face is puffy and blotchy. There is half a leaking breast hanging out one side and the wretched machine pumping away at the other. She looks at you ignoring the lot and beams. You semi-smile back just happy to see people you know, even in this sad state. You didn't always see eye to eye with these women, but you are grateful for what they did that day and the genuine love they shone onto your boy throughout the years.

Suddenly, a beautiful calm aura fills the room. You turn to the doorway and cry some more. This is a happy cry. It's Bestie. You're 99% sure she too is wearing a cape. It's blue with her favourite frangipanis and she seems more kick-arse powerful than normal.

"Oh, thank fCk," you whisper, knowing she can hear your relief with her super senses.

Head on over for some nurturing vibes and safety.

GO TO: PAGE 59

PAGE 35: SOLDIER ON

(from page 28 & 45)

Rather, you hobble on questioning with every step why your presence is necessary. Couldn't you just send the piss test via pigeon? Apparently not. Damn sugar levels. You curse the ridiculously regular appointments as a familiar rustle calls out from your bag.

"Yoo hoooo! Little treaty for the sweetie!"

It's the bullets bitching for attention. You're a bit over random shit suddenly developing the gift of speech and scrunch the deliciously moreish lollies down to the graveyard of bobby pins, tampons and crusty cack that no longer has an earthly term. Not even chocolate will distract the laborious task of heaving yourself into this hospital. Besides, there's a good chance those sweeties are going to tip you into gestational diabetes if you don't reign them and *Lik-Wid-Choc* issue in real soon.

You waddle on despising every step. Having to fill your bladder, hold that amount of urine *and* walk is a fairly big ask. You also swear there can be no movement for hours – to the point where you start prodding your guts just to make sure bub is okay, but the second you've got a litre of liquid to contain the kid takes up synchronised swimming. You probe him and whisper,

"I love you, but my bladder ain't a diving board."

At the reception desk they all but brand you with a scorching hot stamp on your bovine bounty. Wanting an epidural comes at a hefty price. You never fully appreciated the lovely short wait times and calming atmosphere of the PRIMAL WOMB HOUSE, until you come crashing down to the reality of the BIRTHING FARM FACTORY. Actively choosing an epidural-free birth apparently deserves some sort of deranged respect. The drugless birther is rewarded with a comfortable, non-complicated, stress-free experience and a pregnancy paved with every convenience and nicety they can afford you. Delights like spacious suites, multiple guests and control over the air con (which you will discover is actually a big deal) are generously rolled out. True, there is a TONNE of non-numbed pain involved, but hey it comes with a private courtyard!

You, however, chose to walk away from such blissful service **and** to the sacred gift that is your drug-free birth-giving capabilities. From your *shunning* – the universe has taken *that* choice very personally. It is deeply offended by your veering onto a self-paved path and plans on punishing you with a whole lot of pain anyway. Physical and mental. The fun punch starts today.

You kiss goodbye the sweet memories where darling birds chirped and womanly worshipping abounded at the PRIMAL WOMB HOUSE. The polite and welcoming space was a reliable crutch in the lead up to the agonising, drugless torture that awaited you. How you will miss the welcoming tones of the *Vagina V-Force* and their sing-songy melodies.

"Good morning, Mrs Man! Let us help you beautiful Mummy to be! Glorious drug-free warrior! A la natural birther! Wonderful wonder of a womber!"

Those were the days. This new place pales in comparison. The clouds hover twenty four seven and most of your interactions so far consist of no-nonsense, tired, understaffed, underpaid, overworked personnel who are barely going through the motions. A solid pointing system is in place and there is much finger flapping. Toilet → There. → Wheelchair → There. Assistance? → Bahahahaha! No one moves much and seeing as there are a million women in the same situation as you, there is very little hands-on interaction. It makes sense. The staff would be wheelchair bound in a week if they tended to all those waiting room preggo's and their individual woes.

A receptionist raises an eyebrow as you approach. At first you think it's odd and check your clothes. You've gone a floral skirt with an elastic waist. It's a kick arse ensemble, but she still looks at you strangely. Perhaps it's a bit bright? It is an overcast day and maybe you just stand out like the fabulous pork-pie-fashionista you are. You smile anyway as the weird pain strikes again and you clutch frantically at what was formerly your pelvic region. The receptionist gets up and for a second you think she's coming to help. You reach your arm out graciously. She walks straight past it and you nearly fall flat on your misjudgement. Even though it really fricken hurts and concerns for your buckly jelly legs grow, you suck it up, slow your pace and regain balance from the ghost arm that never was. You don't want to complain, or (stupidly) don't want to look needy in front of the entire reception and conclude that staff no doubt become a little immune to achy, flaky, moany Mums-to-be. Still, lately you've noticed the bar for pregnant women in general has risen to a concerning height, particularly for those at the stage where slowing down is recommended. You are days off the nine month mark, but even at the eleventh hour you can't help but feel an invisible pressure to zip it and manage quietly. You wonder when *heavily pregnant women can still do it all!* became a blanket slogan everyone is expected to champion with unbridled enthusiasm *and* still have their wits intact by the mythical end of it all. When did having a baby become so full on? Why is it we have to get to the point of pre-eclampsia, or a threat to ourselves, or the baby's life before it's acceptable to rest without judgement?

"They don't do pregnancy like they used to," a seasoned colleague states one day.

"Pretty sure the methods haven't changed that much," another challenges.

"Nah. Too much pressure and fuffin' about. You lot aren't allowed to just be pregnant. Too many balls in the air."

You find yourself agreeing… in part. It's a dangerous concept for pregnant women to think complaining will result in ridicule and one you are regretfully experiencing. You've been scolded repeatedly for failing to inform medical staff of issues because you don't want to seem *soft and whiny*. Sadly, once you leave the protective shield of professionals (who constantly see the results of *doing it all*) and re-enter the real world, the pressure to conform is just easier. Comments like:

"Women give birth every day. You'll be right…" are not remotely helpful for the over-thinking, over-worrying mind of a first time Mum (or any Mum at any stage). Nor is the far too frequently thrown around and king of insults –

"You're not incapable. You're just pregnant."

Cheers. So glad you cleared that up.

You sketch up a few haiku ideas for a tattoo –

> *Pregnant woman rests * Does not equal laziness * Mind own business*

OR

> *Knowing your limits * During life or pregnancy * Is just sensible*

OR

> *Did I even ask? * Shove opinion up your arse * Too talky turkey*

They may be a tad wordy. Lucky you have long limbs and zero short memory storage and forget the venture two seconds later.

Sadly, it takes a lot of people-pleasing stupidity before you take your own advice. An ignorant few dare say this to you when you take a break longer than normal, or decline social events, or accept help after months of carrying on with life whilst creating life and carrying the heavy load of that life which is equivalent to a small, jaggedy hippopotamus that brushes up on its fencing skills against the inside of your stomach every ten minutes. Where you frequently struggle to stand, let alone walk and just getting out of chairs seems to pierce your spine.

Those who drop the *"You're only pregnant"* comment do so only once (she says like the *Mother* of all mythical fire breathing creatures who just charred the *Town of Too-Much-Talky* to the ground). Not to take anything away from any preggo at any stage who can do it all right up to the crowning moment with little to no issue. They rule. Unfortunately, you're not one of them.

However, thinking someone was coming to your aid in a sea of women in just as much discomfort as you – has you feeling like a right tit and the embarrassment of making a presumption so obvious is a bit too much. Like waving frantically at an old friend who actually isn't an old friend, rather a complete stranger who looks at you like your head is made of marshmallows and it's on fire. That was the look the receptionist gave you. Like she was bored with another vessel, with another issue pawing toward her for help. A look of –

"Deal with it, lady. You're a number in the crowd."

Point taken. You can hack it. You are mobile enough – just.

You hobble on toward the desk, ignoring the standard cheek flush that comes with your constant public humiliations. Focus on the positives – like a pat on the back for making an early appointment. Fool. You soon learn that an *early appointment* does not mean you'll be in and out like the good ole days of last week. You'll see the sun rise and fall twice before your labia gets a look in here.

At least this receptionist is happy to offer hope with a polite veil of bullshit. *You* know it's bullshit. *She* knows it's bullshit. Every jersey cow in the room knows it's bullshit. But it's nice bullshit. It's a bullshit you appreciate.

"Good morning. I'm Mrs Man. I have an 8:15 appointment."

"Okay. We're running a bit behind so just take a seat. It'll be awhile."

"How long is *awhile*?"

"Could be twenty minutes. Could be an hour. Probably more."

"*Mint.* Even with an early appointment?"

"Sorry doll, it doesn't make a difference," she informs you with a lovely smile and → beyond your shoulder. You look around at the wall to wall ocean of bellies that seems to go on for days. When in the shit did these women book their appointments for – three in the morning? It's like a refugee checkpoint for roly-poly dolls. You plonk yourself down into a chair you can barely squeeze in or out of and stare with disbelief. You imagine a post-apocalyptic scene. You have all been handpicked for a special intergalactic colonisation mission. This is the terminal and you and every conceivable walk of life are waiting to embark a rocket bound for Mars.

That's one step for Woman… and one wobbly step… for Bellykind.

You wink like a fully-fledged lunatic at a hugely pregnant woman. She can barely move, but miraculously hauls herself to the only free seat far, far away from you. Whatever. You pick up a magazine and flick through the fashion trends of 1988 and clench the wee that is desperate to escape. You can't move. You can't risk missing this slot. Who knows how long you may have to wait. A crony looking lady with white hair stares at you like she's reading your mind. You presume she is someone's Nan. She is not. Freaky wizard woman has a gutsful and you wonder in what century she booked her appointment.

Just hell no on all levels.

You can't unsee that situation, but you can visualise your bladder traipsing through a hot, dry desert and clench down hard.

GO TO: PAGE 86

PAGE 36: GO HOME

(from page 52)

You know a bit of social respite would definitely be the ticket, but you can feel the bubbling emotions just below your sallow skin, still weary from morning sickness. You hug it out and graciously decline. Bestie hugs you back tight and reassures you she is only a phone call away – while subliminally telling you not to be a hero and suffer alone. You're a sensitive soul at the best of times and the addition of wayward hormones is sabotaging your already fragile stability. You squeeze her hand.

"I'll be right," you offer. She nods knowing full well you won't, but leaves you to it – with all the burdens – with all the loads – with all the constant pretending that you, her and everyone else are keeping it together, keeping up appearances, keeping up the *show*. The truth is – you're tired of the *show*. You've lived a lifetime of the *show*. You need a break from the *show*. The *show* has nearly sent you round the twist so many times you've lost count. You are so over the fCking *show*.

So you lock yourself away and surrender to your mind that insists on drowning you with every sorrowful outcome and you try really, really hard not to fall too deep into that ever familiar, dark and cavernous space of the anti-show realm.

GO TO: PAGE 101

PAGE 37:
THE NURSERY IS DONE!

(from page 11)

People you might normally reach out to are getting busier with Christmas functions and out-of-town family won't be here for a few more weeks. You almost convince yourself that you could paint the nursery, but thankfully the voices took a unanimous vote that – NO – you probably shouldn't. It's a bit sad that the homecoming you envisioned for your little lumpy will be a lacklustre affair. Never mind. In the grand scheme of things it really isn't that important considering he'll be next to your bed for the first few months.

As you open the nursery door the stench of paint hits you hard. You gasp excitedly, almost choking on the fumes and step inside. It's painted! The curtains are up, windows are tinted, blinds hang, hooks are hooked, DIY art displayed, furniture erected and placed where you'd sketched a shitty rough plan six months before, the million dollar cot is assembled and an Ikea puppy rests on the new plush bedding – like a surprise cherry atop the procrastination flavoured cake. The stark, lifeless room is full of warmth and decorated with all the sweet little touches you had piled up and abandoned all hope for.

You sense someone behind you and there is Green Man smiling sheepishly. You cry. He cries. You hug him. He hugs you back. You kiss him lovingly. He cops a feel. You frown. He throws you a metaphorical bone. You roll your eyes. He raises his. You shake your head side to side. He shakes his up and down. You give him the

"*Is no moment sacred?*" speech. He counteracts with –

"Howz about a little nursery slap and tickle?"

You consider the slap bit and refuse to do the nasty in your unborn child's room.

"Be adventurous," he says and you suggest he go be adventurous with his hand. He is immune.

"Just me standing here without toppling is adventurous enough."

"It'll be fun," he continues and you remind him emergency services and a forklift to get you off the ground won't be. He realises he's losing you and grabs your hand smooching it romantically. You embrace again and it's a deliciously lovey dovey moment with the husband you know and adore. Though it's most likely the big whiff of paint messing with your head, you reason the poor bastard hasn't had a shred of intimacy in a long while, so you squeeze his hand and nod.

"Holy fCk! Does that mean yes?"

"Yeah okay. But, let's do it in our bed, just to be safe."

"YES!" he fist pumps and you giggle.

Off you pop to the boudoir and *Reader* – if you're expecting tales of flipping erotica forget it! The only riveting kiss and tell vagina action found on these pages are all reproductive related and ones where babies are exiting.

Green Man gives a five-star effort, but with your clueless land mass involved it's nothing but fifty shafts of mediocrity.

GO TO: PAGE 62

PAGE 38:
ELEPHANT BABY

(from page 58)

YOU should have gone in the wheelchair. You grossly underestimate the distance and your lack of speed and realise you are by no means going to heal *that* quickly. A superhero you are not, so put the bloody cape away – you'll need it for the toddler years.

The angel guides you through the mini maze of cribs mostly filled with tiny, premature infants. The place is bustling, but not full. The sight of these dear little bubs makes you eager to locate your not so little babe. You hear him before you see him and he is crying in despair, again. You rush to pick him up and wonder why he's been left to scream, but quickly adjust your reaction – it's not a daycare centre. You soon find out as a Nurse comes over, (STAFF 1 – *S1*) who seems friendly enough, until she speaks.

"He's a feisty one. He would not let me take his blood," she tells you in an upbeat tone like it's nothing major. You look down at your son's tiny little wrist, heavily bandaged like a burns victim. For once you are lost for words. Green Man steps in.

"I'm sorry, what happened?" he asks, his tone immediately sharp.

"He didn't want me near his hand. He's a bit of a troublemaker," she laughs. At this point, and in her defence, the nurse thinks she's dealing with fairly rational, sound of mind parents. But this, on top of the *Sinister* accusations set the wheels in motion for all to be on guard. You are completely perplexed. Maybe you're hallucinating? You check Green Man. He just looks pissed.

"He's only a few days old. What trouble could he be?" he questions abruptly. Even in your muntation you sense you should intervene.

"Will he be okay?" you quietly ask. She adjusts her casual behaviour about chopping into your baby and offers something resembling excuses. They're limp.

"Oh, it's only a scratch. It will heal quickly."

It must have been more than a scratch to have that amount of gauze, you think, but are still too polite to say out loud.

"Will there be a scar?"

"I doubt it and if there is it will only be a little one. As he grows it will disappear... you know... it'll stretch out," she offers nervously as it finally seems to sink in how on edge you really are.

"It looks pretty bad," you say, and she puts her hand on your shoulder.

"He'll be fine. They heal quick. He's a healthy little man."

"Exactly! When can we take him home?" you snap. Her eyes widen as she fumbles for his chart.

"Well, I took his bloods pretty much as soon as he came down. Now they just need to run the tests and then we'll know for sure."

"If he has a *sinister*?"

"They're testing for all sorts," she responds awkwardly and looks down at the floor.

"But that's the main one, right? That's why we've been forced down here instead of taking him home?" You bulldoze now.

"It's one of them," she reluctantly replies.

"I can tell you now he's negative."

"It's just precautionary and hopefully he'll be fine to go when the tests come back," *S1* feigns a positive air in an attempt to dismiss your interrogation. She fusses with the clipboard. You are developing a deep disdain for clipboards.

"When will that be? We've got family arriving today who want to see him. Should we go home and come back in a few hours?" you naively ask and she actually laughs at the suggestion.

"Oh no. It won't be that quick! Earliest will be next week and even that's a stretch as a lot of staff are away."

"What?" you raise your voice now and Green Man steps back in as does another staff member (STAFF 2 – *S2*). She looks irritated by the interaction and soon makes the extent of her irritation abundantly clear.

"The test results can take anywhere up to a week and they're short staffed, so there is really no point in you coming back today as you'll just have to go home again without him," she snaps short and sharp.

"I can't believe this is happening. There is nothing wrong with him," you blurt, riddled with panic. *S2* remains calmly adamant.

"Mrs Man, I understand you're upset, but we have procedures in place we must follow."

"What about feeding?" Green Man asks as he strokes your arm.

"She can express some now to leave and continue overnight. You can come early in the morning if you like when he'll probably be due for more."

"So... I can't feed him myself? He has to have a bottle already? Can't I stay?" you plead through the tears you are no longer embarrassed to release.

"I'm afraid there are a lot of families from the country who have been flown in, so all the housing is occupied. Some mothers can't even get here and..." she goes on to list many tales of sincere woe that are truly more sorrowful and direr than yours. You feel like a right arsehole and are convinced she's doing her best to make sure that you do. Once again your exhausted mind battles between guilt and anger for your child being wrongly incarcerated, forced to spend a night alone with strangers and separated from you.

"I don't need a bed. Could I just sit here? I won't get in the way," you whisper through more tears and even you are shocked at the childlike desperation in your voice. You never hear her answer. Green Man intervenes putting his arm around you and leans in close.

"It's just one night. Better you get a full night's sleep and we'll come in early tomorrow," he suggests soothingly. He knows your reaction will be the same, but you appreciate his efforts. Green Man and the staff move away to talk without you, sharing a mutual respect of belonging to the *sound-of-mind-club*. Your membership approval is pending. You watch the blurry, rational scene and suddenly feel like a filthy, infected, mentally unstable desperado. You admit defeat. Every professional in the room knows why you are here and whether or not you're imagining it, it feels like they have all passed a guilty verdict upon the three of you. Clearly everything would be less awkward if you'd just bugger off home, so they can begin de-cluttering and decontaminating their workspace. The place really is void of staff and the ones who are there seem eager for you, your questions and your merry band of supposedly diseased, bed-hogging company to just go and let them tend to worthier patients.

You clumsily express and feed bub for the last time that day. You hold him close. You do not want to leave. It feels as if you can't leave. You drag it out until even Green Man presses you to make a move. *S1* tries to offer something resembling comfort, but you've entered a space where no one else is welcome. A place where only you and your baby exist. The tears that never really left return along with an intense amount of bitterness. You wipe them off baby's face as you kiss him endlessly and reluctantly put him back into the crib. It's the most painful thing you have ever had to do.

You look at the other babies and back at your healthy little man. He looks like an elephant. You kiss his sweet head, breathe in his scent one final time and exit the space like a zombie, leaving Green Man to gather the details. As you walk through the corridors with empty hands it feels as if you have experienced some form of death. You know how ridiculous this thinking is knowing that maybe somewhere in the hospital some poor parents are suffering such a fate. You also know that *you* should be grateful that your child is alive and healthy. That *you* will see him in the morning unlike the other Mothers whose precious infants will have to spend months away from them. You feel sickened by your self-pity and descend deeper into the dark. Families wait in the reception with their flowers and luggage and the actual child they gave birth to. They are so joyful. So elated. So complete and you utterly despise them all. Normal you, even when in a place of sadness can muster up an appreciative smile for other's happiness. Not this version. You are numb. You feel nothing. You don't know what to do. It feels like the worse come down ever known from a five-day bender. A good time that only involved getting high off your baby and definitely not catching a *Sinister*.

DO YOU:
A) FALL IN A HEAP: PAGE 19
B) HEAD HOME: PAGE 74

PAGE 39:
B) LOSE YOUR BANANA

(from page 9)

You lose it completely. Tropically. You start throwing whatever isn't nailed to the floor. Security are called to hold you down for sedation. You are so drugged up you slip into a mild coma waking up in a drooling puddle in your home.

"Where is the baby?" you scream.

"Right next to you. Just stay calm. You're home now," Green Man soothes you. He is doing something randomly out of character like a Sudoku, or baking, or putting things back where they actually belong. Something is definitely not right.

"Did he have a growth? A disease? A terminal illness?" you pepper hysterically.

"What? No. Chill!"

"Oh, thank goodness," you say, relieved and pick bub up who coos and nuzzles into your chest.

The Christmas tree is glorious, and the house is full of love and festive cheer. Life is perfect and forever will be. You look outside at the passing spaceships and thank your lucky stars for this glorious, stress-free home of yours – *Planet Breakdown*. Nanoo nannot.[3]

Oh sweet pancake-head. Float here a bit before you return to reality.

GO TO: PAGE 58

---

[3] *Robin Williams' brilliant mind*

PAGE 40:
B) PULL UP YOUR BIG GIRL PANTS

(from page 95)

Way to go you amazing thing and good for you. Unfortunately, as wonderful as this bravery train is this was not to be your fate. Even if you did commit, you were destined to be numbed and in the end it's all out of your control. There is no choice but to administer a spinal block for the life of your baby, who was and is fine.

The cosmic joke is you are about to pay for that pain relief. Things are going to get dysfunctional.

GO TO: PAGE 6

PAGE 41:
B) LET HIM GO

(from page 16, 82 & 104)

Oh dear. It appears red wine is all your Uncle has left in the cabinet and your cousins want to pickle the Father-to-be. A lot of whetting of the baby's head ensues. Chants of *"You're fCked now mate! You're fCked now mate!"* are sung out with drunken gusto along with taunts that neither rhyme, nor have an iota of logical thought put into them. You make a note to flick your cousins in the ear when next they are sober and forget the malice three seconds later. It would be a long, long wait anyway. Before you know it Green Man is being dragged to the car like an inebriated baby foal, all gooey and wobbly.

Back home he gets a second wind. He opens another bottle of wine and proceeds to play a Dave Matthews concert full bore and then passes out wearing a Viking helmet, mullet wig and coconut titties. Poor lamb must have made a last ditch effort for some sort of inebriated role play. You take off his shoes, pull up the blankets and oddly don't mind dealing with any of it. You'll be doing it for real soon enough, though thankfully to an infant.

Your back is aching way more than usual. A hot shower should do the trick. It does. You pop your elephant apparatus wear on, double check the hospital bag and hop into bed. As you lay your head on the pillow a blissful feeling of peaceful joy and warmth washes over you and you fall into a happy hippo-like sleep. This is short lived. The warmth you feel is your waters breaking. The baby is finally coming!

GO TO: **PAGE 90**

PAGE 42: OVERACHIEVING NONG

(from page 63 & 81)

You end up in hospital admitted into the MORON section where the Nurses line up in droves to chastise your piss-poor judgement and woeful self-negligence. It's like a scene from a gang movie where everyone comes to claim their vengeance and all this lot are missing are some batons and knuckle busters. Every member on staff has something to say about your stupidity and you swear it's been put over the PA as they just keep coming.

Thankfully, the baby is fine, but you have to stay overnight for observation and twenty four hours' worth of scolding. It doesn't stop there. Family and friends either come to visit, or phone in their comments. It's like a telethon for idiocy with people pledging their donations of rational thinking because clearly you are without yours. Suffice to say you've learned your lesson and will never again attempt such a solo feat – at least not while heavily pregnant.

Your decorated home remains so until Green Man – who is forced to call his work trip short – returns to take it all down. He knows better than to lecture you in your current state, but for the few days after there is much head shaking and disapproving sighs as he begrudgingly waits on your now permanently bed-ridden self.

Soooo much still to do and you're as useful as a parachute made from last decades fishnets. You fool.

GO TO: PAGE 23

PAGE 43:
B) BABY SHOPPING

(from page 85 & 106)

Time for the fun stuff. You plot, plan and connive to convince Green Man it is not necessary for him to accompany you on any of the baby shopping. He stubbornly strokes his beard and is irritatingly immune to your wool pulling.

"Nice try," he quips, scooping his arm around your growing waist and escorting you to the car. Poo.

Baby shopping in baby shops is very akin to the whole high-end clothes caper. Rather wroughtable. To combat this, you've embarked on a nursery campaign reasoning away every purchase with a few catchy slogans.

"This is my first-ever-baby!" you sing, until Green Man's ears bleed. If he needs real hard convincing, you'll chuck in a shameless, *"I've been waiting my whole life for this!"* and other first Mum clichés. You even get some t-shirts made up –

FIRST EVER BABY!

Unfortunately, your breasticles stretch it out so badly it reads –

FIST EVERY BODY!

Oh dear. A few disgusted glances from fellow shoppers and Green Man offers his jumper to hide your shame. You both move on.

It's cot time. You know exactly which one you want and yay it just happens to be part of a matching three piece set with drawers and a change table. What are the very unresearched odds of that? You flutter about trying to distract Green Man from the price tag, not that he is single-handedly footing the bill. At this point you are still roaming free with the non-children folk, able to make a living with abandon and cluelessly enjoying the freedom of working without compromises. Still naively in love with the illusion that when baby comes you will maintain a career without handing over most of your wage to fund the costs of having both a baby and a career. The career that you'll eventually have to give up because you're essentially paying your employer to work for them due to all that selfish baby-having and needy career...ing. Silly sausage.

Despite the inner picketing, you are not without coin yet and are ready to invest. After all – *FIST EVERY BODY*... oops... *FIRST EVER BABY!* You lower your *power to the people* pose, zip the borrowed jumper up to your neck and continue the buttery rouse. It's not working. Green Man is gone. Turns out not far. He's just passed out on the floor with one hand clutching his heart, the other holding a price tag. People have gathered around him. You glance at his chest which rises and falls and continue browsing. You've seen it all before with most purchases. Wedding rings, furniture, houses, pets, vacations and recently at a swanky Japanese restaurant when he had to be Heimliched after reading the bill. Out flew a bit of sixty dollar regurgitated teriyaki Angus and for a second you thought he was going to have another crack – just to get his money's worth. That was a fun night. Naturally none of this comes as a surprise and you figure the lie down will do him good. He should probably recharge anyway for when you announce you've already purchased the three piece set. You look around the shop for a defibrillator just in case, but only see a fire extinguisher. Close enough. You can always foam him back to consciousness if need be.

Over to the prams and your fingers tingle. It's like shopping for a new car and there are sooooo many! The price tags range from *beer-budget* to *average-humans-disintegrate-upon-looking.* You head to the middle where you are spoiled for choice. Then you see it. A heavy-duty-off-road-all-terrain-girthy-sexy-muther-of-a-tri-wheeler and you immediately know you are destined to spend many glorious head-fCking years together. You will get up close and personal with this thing cleaning out shit, spew, shlop, vom and elements that defy reason and require an exorcist to rid from the planet. It will cradle and transport your babies long after they should reasonably be using a pram. You'll glide over insane terrains, whip in and out of shopping centres like a swat vehicle. It's going to move through sand, mud, gravel, rivers, oceans and places that technically should not be inhabited by pram, let alone humans.

It will act as the perfect seat to rest your weary arse in the coming years of fetes, markets, shows and festivals. Even when that hip-ship has long sailed you'll convince yourself that with this uberness of mobility under your baby's belt – your cool-o-meter will justify a middle-aged strut amongst the youthy people. You picture yourself casually leaning on its sturdy handle, donning an ill-fitting op-shop frock, necking an $85 parsley & catnip infused craft beer, buckled over and panting after dancing for 1.6 minutes in the brutally abusive sun unseen by your kid-consumed eyeballs for a child-rearing aeon. Concerned youngsters will gather to sponge you down.

"I'm fine. Let's rock this shit!" you'll slur like an ageing hippie at a twenty five and under rave.

Even with all this humiliation to come – you are utterly in love with every one of these delusions that will clearly only happen with this purchase. Mountain Buggy Ethereal Adventure Hipster Baby? Hell effing yeah! At least your kid will be cool.

You look up at the floor to ceiling promo poster of bullshit fit couples tra la laaing through the forest with their perfect baby and their perfect lives and smile back at them. Yes. Thy will be done.

The visions are as powerful as the marketing and there is nothing that can stop this transaction now. You must have this pram. You reach for the price tag and nearly choke on your tongue. Nothing can justify the amount this thing costs. Poof go your daydreams up in a cloud of unicorn-rainbow-baby-earth-mother-goddess-flowy-midriff-flower-crowned-boho-trendy-catnip-craft-beer smoke. Pooey.

GO TO: PAGE 48

PAGE 44:
CONGRATS ON 12 WEEKS

(from page 98)

You couldn't quite do the traditional hush-hush until the three-month mark thing, so that ship rapidly sailed. You barely made it to three minutes after you got confirmation, but none of that matters now. Time for the fun stuff of meeting your little miracle and hearing the heartbeat! Hopefully, it will extract a heartbeat from your husband who seems to be burrowing deeper into the sandpit of denial. Thankfully, he's popped out for a bit and is behaving semi-normal for this exciting moment.

Holding your hand tight, he strokes your forehead and steals a kiss whenever the technician looks back at the monitor. You cry. Green Man cries. The ultrasound lady cries. There is so much blubbering joy as your little blob bobs in time to the heartbeat in all its three month glory, which suddenly increases as she hones in on one spot of your tum. She switches back and forth from you to the monitor pushing, prodding, twisting, typing and the joyful vibe in the room dissipates. She's measuring something and she's measuring it a lot, so of course you come to the direst of conclusions.

"Is something wrong?" you ask.

"I'm not sure. Have you received your blood tests yet?"

"They're being sent to my doctor. We're seeing him after you."

"Okay, good. I'll send these through to him now."

"Why? Is something wrong?" you repeat.

"It could be nothing and it's difficult to tell at this early stage. We just need to make sure that bub is developing at a certain rate for the time frame," she offers, then looks over at your face that has instantly turned white. She brings her chair closer to you. "Don't be too concerned. We just need to take precautions," she says kindly, but vague. An uneasiness washes over you and houses itself beneath your skin. You immediately take up nail-biting.

The trip to your doctor tests your nerves a little more as he too concludes they should veer on the side of caution. Your blood results have returned and are showing high levels of some bloody hormone that warrants the need for high level precautionary measures because you are thirty four years of age and in the wrinkly-ass danger zone. In other words *the paranoia category* where anything remotely imperfect is tested and long waits of not-knowing are endured. Nothing is immediate in this world and unfortunately patience has never been a virtue of yours. This paired with a default thinking of worst-case scenarios does not a calm state make.

It's been recommended your decrepit old self should get an *amniocentesis* test. A big ole bastard needle of gloom you will soon come to loathe as much as the term "cover all bases."

Green Man comes through with calm and support. Unfortunately, he can't make it to the appointment, so you decide to ask your Besties.

But which one will you take?

A) CHILD FREE BESTIE: PAGE 108
B) BESTIE WITH A BABY: PAGE 52

PAGE 45:
PARKING AT THE HOSPITAL

(from page 6 & 99)

Booking into the main hospital was a lot easier than expected requiring minimal evil plotting. Getting into the actual building itself is a whole other story. Parking at a hospital in a heavily condensed suburb is just a cruel, bloody joke when you're a woolly mammoth with a full bladder. But, you finally manage to jag a spot only made possible because you thrust your twitchy eyeball at a tiny couple so old – they may very well have been driving a horse and cart. You stare them down until they have no choice but to relent. You know you're being incredibly unreasonable and slightly psychotic, but you are so, so tired for social niceties.

To add to the fun, the stabbing pain that brutalises your pelvis like a pitchfork occurs every couple of steps now. What is essentially a five minute trip takes you nearly twenty five and you're not even close to the entrance yet. You question the parking and endeavour to pen an email to the town planner suggesting they don a birth suit, fill it with bricks and have someone kick them in the crotch every few metres just so they can appreciate the full extent of their piss-poor designs. None of this will do any good as the poor town planner has been dead in his grave over a hundred and fifty years and you forget the lot barely half a second later.

You consider wagging the appointment.

DO YOU:

A) WAG IT: PAGE 28
B) SOLDIER ON: PAGE 35

PAGE 46: DRIVE YOURSELF TO HOSPITAL

(from page 13 & 103)

Green Man appears at the doorway like a late night hamburger shlopping all over the show. He pauses against the bricks and proceeds to hurl over the lilly pillies. Chunky bits of god knows what hang from the poor leaves now dripping in putrid bile and all you do is smile. You notice he's holding something other than himself against the wall. It's a towel – a good one and a rare non-Kmart item – worshipped for its plush smooshiness and mystifying thread count. You handpicked these babies for the wedding registry and only ever roll them out to impress guests. Green Man had his chance with them, but copped a lifetime ban soon after the great dog-washing-with-the-non-two-buck-shop-towel debacle. There is a good chance he may sop up his digrace using this sacred cloth and *still* you do not waiver from the psychotic grinning.

"Are you okay?" you ask, genuinely concerned.

"He'll be fine. Hop in and sit down before another contraction comes," your Mum's reason rings with calm determination, even if it smells of wine. You descend your leaky bounty onto the fresh leather seat when suddenly the towel is abruptly shoved between you and the car.

"Put this on sss... the sssseat."

"What? Why?"

"No baby juices on the... on tha... new car." The slurred words drool down his chin as his head bobs back and forth, eyes rolling about like confused marbles. Your usual response would be a whole lot of profanities and a string of recommendations to shove the item north of his rectal passage, but any act resembling normalcy has long left this circus.

"I'm padded up! It's fine!"

"Don't c..care... towelll," he insists in full Neanderthal mode.

Meanwhile, your Mum – who has changed her outfit, packed a bag, made a coffee and put on a full face of make-up – awaits on the passenger side looking like a late night Sofia Loren, albeit an over-the-limit version. Normally she would politely ignore Green Man's eccentric ticks, but as previously mentioned "normal" has well and truly run far from this funny farm.

"Don't be ridiculous. Let her get in the car. She's having a bloody baby," she orders in the hopes he will focus on her and forget the towel nonsense. He doesn't and even in his unsteady state swiftly shoves the towel under you before you fall onto the plush, quality seating.

"Yesss... *bloody*... ex... exac... ex-aca-taca-ly! Babis... are... messssy... as... fCkkkk..."

"Honestly," she calls out appalled, plugs in her phone and starts scrolling. Apparently Mum has made a playlist for the occasion and you cross your fingers it isn't *50s Crooners Greatest Hits*. The last thing you need is a drunken rat packy medley triggering Green Man to who knows where.

He ignores your Mum, or is just that drunk he doesn't see her, and staggers around the car somehow plopping himself on the back seat.

"Put your belt on, babe. I can't promise this won't be a bumpy ride."

No answer.

"Bugger him. He'll be fine. Let's go!"

"Mum!"

"My grandson is ready to come out! Don't worry about boozy. He can sleep it off."

You convince her to buckle in the inebriated Father-to-be which she reluctantly does. It then becomes very official –

YOU ARE DRIVING *YOURSELF* TO THE HOSPITAL.

Yayyyyy_{yyyy}.

No big deal. It could be way worse. You had a friend whose labour came on so quick she didn't even make it to the driveway and delivered her own baby on the edge of a toilet! She never once complained, or made a big deal, or turned her tale into a ridiculously over the top novel wah-wah-wahing over every miniscule inconvenience. Nope. She just spat bub out like she was taking a crap and got on with life. Warrior and forever hero.

The hospital is only twenty seven minutes and thirty one kilometres away. The silver lining is that it is thankfully midnight, so no stress about traffic. Yippee.

And off you go.

WHICH ROUTE WILL YOU TAKE?
A) BACK ROAD: PAGE 89
B) FREEWAY: PAGE 105

PAGE 47:
B) PRIVATE HOSPITAL

(from page 21)

You take the private hospital tour. Green Man has developed an invisible rash he scratches frantically at. He sighs heavily, taking it all in like a twitchy calculator. You ignore him and twirl like a swollen Von Trapp. This place is better than a hotel.

"I don't know if we can afford this," he whispers hotly and not remotely in the good way. He looks like an ostrich who just had a car accident and forgot to renew his insurance. He fidgets desperately next to a statue of the virgin Mary, bringing his hands up in prayer.

"You're not religious," you remind him.

"Never too late to join up," he replies.

"It's not like a gym membership."

"I'm willing to give anything a crack if it stops your delusions."

"Just let me have this moment," you sing and continue spiralling. You visualise a reality where the majestic birth of your first born takes place on a fluffy, painless cloud amongst these beautiful surrounds. You breathe in the stench of disinfectant and float back down, landing with the heaviness of poverty. He looks at you nervously. You stroke your invisible beard. It's a tricky decision. Green Man's mental health, or your cushiness? This is a toughie.

WHAT WILL IT BE?
A) GREEN MANS WELLBEING: PAGE 102
B) YOUR OVERPRICED WELLBEING: PAGE 98

PAGE 48:
COOCHIE COO – WHO'S A SEXY PRAM?

(from page 43)

A muffled voice speaks from under the jumper. *"Do it!"*

"Listen to the shirt! Fist it up," the hoodie chimes in. Great. The clothes are talking again. You give your chest a slap, rip off the price tag and start pacing near the "nursing chairs". This is going to be challenging and even you with your shocking sense of spending can't think of how to convince G-Man to depart with his lucky charms. Suddenly a haze of rational thinking and sensible money handling fills the air. Green Man has risen. You quickly pocket the price tag before he can see it.

***

YOU: How was that then?

HIM: Brilliant.

YOU: I knew you couldn't hack it.

HIM: I can hack it fine. Just got a little woozy… and there was a bit of a misunderstanding.

YOU: What misunderstanding?

HIM: Some lady thought I'd passed out.

YOU: You did pass out.

HIM: Only for a second. I didn't need resuscitating.

YOU: Get some action did ya?

HIM: Think I got tongued by a pregnant woman. She went into labour and they've taken her to hospital.

YOU: You still got it.

HIM: I never lost it.

YOU: Indeed. Nothing sexier than a fainty man passed out in a baby warehouse. Rowrlll!

HIM: Hmf. What are you looking at?

YOU: Prams.

HIM: I see that. Which one?

YOU: That one.

Green Man looks up and down the line. You sense him crunching numbers and weighing up every variable to justify spending what he has worked out in seconds is costly. But, you've got a secret weapon. The handy thing about ex-mechanics is that it never leaves them. It's within their nature to meticulously suss shit out and lucky for you Green Man is a sucker for quality and secretly a little showy. You might actually be in with a chance and shamelessly play to his ego, manically scrolling reviews that are thankfully all five star – no surprise considering the cost.

He spends the next forty eight minutes looking the vehicle over from handle to wheel. You leave him to it. Your presence has an anti-purchase vibe and you want him to think this was all his doing. The *ego* card. Shameless wifey strategy 101.

But, does he buy any of it?

GO TO: PAGE 7

PAGE 49:
PRIVATE HOSPITAL HOTEL

(from page 70)

You are rolled into something resembling a hotel room and pinch yourself you could be this lucky. That is until you attempt to sleep. As you fall into a deep slumber, the night shift kicks in. It seems to combat a late shift the staff behave like it's a day shift. They talk at volumes that defy the sound barrier and laugh voraciously like they're doing tequila shots from bedpans. They call out across the long halls and have a good old catch up. It's all very social and joyous and you reason it's most likely the position of your room making it seem louder than it probably is. Perhaps you're in the highway *hotspot*. You are not. You give them the benefit of doubt. Even though allowing Mums to go into a deep sleep only to wake them up sporadically throughout the entire night seems like a cruel form of torture – the staff are most likely oblivious they're doing it and no doubt all will settle tomorrow. It does not. It just gets worse. You begin to suspect they may be doing it on purpose as a service of not getting Mums too comfortable. Like preparation for the reality to come once they get home. Which is great and one day you'll appreciate the sentiment, but not today.

You wonder if it's you just being dramatic from lack of sleep. You're not. At this hospital partners can also stay, which Green Man does the night you have the baby. He *too* complains about the noise and refuses to return. You nod like you're a little wounded but are secretly thrilled because trying to get comfortable hours after giving birth is hard enough, let alone sharing what is essentially a king single with someone who sleeps spread eagled.

"Naww, I'll miss you (unhappy mouth wave) *Catch ya later bed hog!*"

He may as well have stayed. Even with all the space in the world it makes no difference. Each morning comes with no sleep and a naive hope that tonight will be better. You don't complain. You don't want to ruffle feathers especially as you've apparently been the "perfect patient" and the midwives happily tell you so. They gleefully confide they enjoy the easy going visits with you and little Bumbalina. You puff a little, but once they leave you feel like a gloating fool. You are *so, so, so* exhausted and this mental-baby-brain-blend of yours is like a multi-flavoured thick shake of disintegration. All you want is some uninterrupted rest. One full hour should do it – just to calm your frazzlement and stop the room from flashing for a bit.

Do you get it?

GO TO: PAGE 113

PAGE 50:
THE FINALE

PAGE 51: ROLL UP ROLL UP

(from page 50)

Welcome to the Third Trimester. Good times ahead. Some top features to look forward to: A disturbing Lik-Wid-Choc habit and a ball sniffing fetish along with growing concerns about the birth itself including:

X – Shitting yourself

X – Screaming

X – Doggy style enforcement

X – Epidural refusal

And some things to kiss goodbye for a while and inevitably forever:

X – Views of your feet

X – Painless mobility

X – Full night's sleep

X – Pelvic floor

Shit is about to get real… but hopefully not literally. Let's ignore it all for a bit, shall we?

Pamper time!

WHICH ONE?
A) FRESH GODDESS (to continue baby girl journey): **PAGE 94**
B) THE SHOWER/SHAVE DILEMMA (to continue baby boy journey): **PAGE 104**

PAGE 52:
B) BESTIE WITH A BABY

(from page 44 & 108)

Bestie with a baby (BB) gives you a huge supportive hug. She totally understands your apprehension having gone through the same stress a year before and then some.

BB & BB-SENIOR FLASHBACK

BB's tale is an interesting one. Not only did she take the very rewarding (though mentally draining and financially taxing) path of IVF – she chose to take it alone like the no bullshit, independent warrior she is. When she finally fell pregnant, BB – who had already lost so much and nearly lost herself. She basically died during her labour, but knew nothing of it until months later when her Mum casually slipped it into a conversation whilst chopping carrots for the evening stew. No-one, least of all BB, suspected that level of secret keeping stealth from BB-Senior. Always a crowd favourite and guru to all, no shin-dig is complete without BB's Mum and her wickedly dry sense of humour. This fine Lady is cucumber cool, kind, generous and rarely says no to even the most mental suggestions. Always up for a good laugh, good food, good company and good booze. Her signature drink is a polite cuppa heavily laced with a sneaky splash of scotch that she sips like a demure duchess and none are ever the wiser. She is a top fiver on your heroine list just for the boozy tea and a beloved legend of the people.

So, after witnessing her only daughter essentially flat-line before her eyes, she shelved her emotions and three remaining threads of sanity – to protect BB from any further stress. Talk about a Mother's love. BB, whose random apples do not fall far from the random apple tree, one day casually shares this near-death tale during a pre-preggo Sunday-sesh, that turns into a Monday-hair-of-the-dog-sesh, that morphs into a tune-out-Tuesday-sesh just so you can all process the ordeal. Suddenly your shit seems irrelevant as you recall the hangover. Imagining a world without BB in it was so incomprehensible, you attempted to drink the prospect away. She's another soul mate that fell from the heavens with a crate of wine, an adventurous heart and a loyalty that makes you wonder what you ever did to deserve her friendship. You're fairly sure you're related. You know those people you meet once and have an instant connection to? The epigenetic flashbacks of plowing Irish fields and sharing other medieval misdemeanours with her feel very real, and the freaky-deaky-woo-woo similarities between the two of you are borderline bizarre. Example; your Dad has a dust collecting photo of his golden oldies rugby team. You'd seen this pic a thousand times before, but one day something compelled you to take a closer look. One of the players looked familiar. It was BB's Dad. He knew your Dad years before you and BB had even met. It was the cement that bound the bond of freaky-deaky sisterhood forever.

She's a good googy and you're grateful to have her by your side right now. BB's beautiful bub sleeps soundly in the pram and she's brought enough snacks, toys and distractions to start a daycare centre if bub does awake. Thumbs up. You all enter the room which is unusually dark and rather ominous. The technician reassures you it's to create a relaxed atmosphere as this is a high risk procedure with the worst-case scenario being miscarriage. Basically – don't move so she doesn't fCk it up. You nod agreeably promising to keep as still as the grave. She lubes you up and begins. The room is silent. There is an assistant monitoring a computer and both women are softly spoken. She is just about to inject your belly with a needle fit for a dinosaur when Bestie's little Beastie awakens and not with a quiet whimper – more wild safari wailing. Everyone in the room shudders, especially you. Thankfully the doctor has steady handed reflexes and enough sense to know when to step back. She is iridescent and the assistant rushes over, probably with some smelling salts. Your friend delivers a string of heavily whispered profanities as she too darts to her darling foghorn. She shoves in a dummy and the child immediately falls asleep.

"I'm so sorry. She must have been dreaming," she apologises, red in the face.

"Apparently of a buffalo stampede," you comment and burst into laughter. It's a while before everyone is composed and even longer before your jelly-belly calms its wibble-wobble. The heaviness of the situation soon returns as you face the inevitable task you wish would just be over and done with. BB senses your concern and reaches out to hold your hand. Again, Bestie with a baby is the psychic rock who sees through your crap efforts of poorly convincing others you're okay. She always knows when you're not and as you squeeze her hand, a tidal wave of love and admiration for this gift of a friend washes over you. You can't help but be impressed that after the obscene amount of alcohol the two of you have consumed collectively over the years, that either one of you even knows who the other is. Many a brain cell has been lost and while it will be more noticeable once baby brain settles in – you regret nothing. Especially not the mojitos. She makes a mean mojito and visions of mint leaves, lime wedges and woefully calculated pours of rum soon dance across your skin.

"Where have you gone?" BB watches you trance out.

"The mojitos are dancing. They're really good," you answer. She immediately grins and plays along seamlessly, letting you think your weird shit is normal.

"Righto. Well, how about you come back now? We can watch them later," Bestie says softly, rubbing your hand again. She knows you're scared and appreciates the creative distraction you've allowed yourself.

"Oh, alright. If I must," you answer and flash a cheesy. She grins wider and gives you a wink. The beautiful, patient technicians gently smile. Even though the circumstances are sour, the moment between you four women in this dark, ominous room is comforting and you adore the unspoken reassurance from each of them. You will come across these strangers time and time again. Sadly, most of them become faceless, but you never forget the sentiments. Anyone who can offer a shred of kindness while injecting bellies with life-threatening needles, or probing a disagreeable uterus, or contorting breasts into balloon shaped animals while still cracking jokes – truly is a gift to this world. You and your bits are sincerely grateful to be selflessly serviced by these angels of community care. And for friends like BB.

The technician is done and sends you off with a limp promise someone will make contact with the results as soon as they can. You deflate once more at the prospect of waiting two weeks. BB doesn't want to leave you in this unsteady state and offers to take you out for lunch.

DO YOU:
A) GO TO LUNCH: PAGE 96
B) DECLINE AND G O HOME: PAGE 36

PAGE 53:
THE WHITE COATS OF CHRISTMAS PRESENT

(from page 110)

Finally, pull rank. You arrive back at the hospital you cannot wait to never return to ever again. There is a nativity scene in the foyer and you pause a moment to reflect on Mary. Religion aside – this chick was Queen of the ill-treated preggo's. Any woman who gives birth surrounded by shit flicking hay and farm fuzz deserves some respect. You throw her a nod and hobble on.

Despite your exhaustion you walk with crystal clear intent. By hook or by crook you are taking your son home, or will get tackled to the ground trying. It's Christmas day and you've brushed your hair, slapped on some makeup and donned a festive dress. Clearly you mean business. You sport a bright Bali frock bought especially for your baby's homecoming and intend to celebrate that moment right now. The mission, the sunny day and the dress seems to clear some of the darkness from your mind.

"Anda terlihat bagus dalam gaun tenda yang elastis!" Of course the clothes are talking again. You are happy to hear them. You smile at the compliment and can't help but agree – you really do *look good in an elastic tent dress*. You make your way over to your cherry puddin-pie and swaddle him to your cheek. His intoxicating smell is like Christmas in a cup and your breasts immediately leak their egg nog.

The staff are still running with an aloof approach – one they couldn't even drop on a day about peace, love and good-bloody-will to all. You refuse to let them spoil your favourite holiday and sweetly sing lame carols into Mini Man's little ear. You've gone into the maternal vortex. Green Man, however is over it. After an hour of being ignored he approaches *S1* who immediately looks on edge.

"Merry Christmas," he offers politely.

"And to you," she quietly says back.

"Any news on the test results?"

"I'm not sure."

"Could you please check?"

"Well, no actually. I've got…" and she lists all the things she no doubt needs to tend to, but Green Man pushes back.

"Yeah look, I appreciate you've got more important things to do, but you rang us. Would it hurt to just have a quick look, or maybe ring someone?" His tone sounds foreign, even to him. *S1* twitches like she's had orders into her earpiece to approach the hostile with caution. Green Man swoops in again. "I get how busy you guys are and I know it's not a priority to what's going on here, but we've got a house full of family who would like to see our son and we just want to know if there's an issue. If he has to stay – fine, but my wife deserves some answers before she completely loses her mind," his voice shakes. He clears his throat to apologise, but the staff have missed the cue. *S1* is speechless by his sudden surge of authority and looks to *S2* who is officially pissed. She glares and launches a firewall from afar.

"We've already explained the process to you, Mr Man. We're doing all we can. You're not the ***only*** family who wants to be home on Christmas day!"

"But we are the *only* family with a kid who shouldn't be here," Green Man fires back. No one yells – it's like an intense battle of the passive-aggressors with neither party backing down. Even though you're pretty much postal at this point – the confrontation sets the tears rolling again. You wipe them on bubs muslin and bury your lips into his troublemaking wound that has nearly healed. Buggery little bastard oxymoron. It doesn't matter. Your decision has been made and nothing will stop you walking out those doors of doom without your child. *S2* must sense your psychosis and looks over just as Green Man rolls up his tongue lashing sleeves.

"I can make a call, but it will have to be later," she snaps again and looks at the computer as if confirming she is far too busy dealing with real life and death situations to service the whims of pushy-pineapple-princess-parents. Of course she is right, though ignoring you all is an approach not well received by Green Man – *Master of Aloofery*. He puts his head down and laughs. It's an odd reaction for him, but it dawns on all who witness it – the man has reached his piss-taken limit. He stares at them. They stare back uneasily. It's like watching a game of phrenetic ping-pong with Green Man the first to retreat. He shakes his head repeatedly, scoffs a little and sighs non-stop for the next ten minutes.

"Sorry, babe. I tried," he says, deflated and kisses bub. You couldn't love him more.

"It's all good. I'm wearing my lucky dress," you respond like some all-knowing guru about to launch a cult. Just as you prepare to make a series of terrible decisions, your Christmas miracle arrives in the form of...

THE WHITECOATS

The following scenes play out like an actual TV drama as a group of doctors and officials float in. They are a cloud of hope. A heavenly force. An apparition with otherworldly timing. You scan their faces and it takes half a second to gauge they are the possible saviours for your *sinister* situation. They move around gooing and gaaing over the few babies dressed in their sweet Christmas get-ups, until they realise there is only one Mother present. They lock you and your sad-sack party in their empathetic sights. One of them immediately reads the extreme despair you're projecting. She radiates goodness and even amid this bizarre ordeal you can't help but be in awe of her. She reminds you of some of your favourite power actresses and much like the characters these women play, this one does not suffer fools, nor foolish situations. Welcome *Doctor H* – the H stands for Heroine.

"Happy holidays to you, new Mum! I love your dress! Very festive," she genuinely loves the dress and her minions all chime along with compliments and nods of praise. You can't blame them. The dress is fricken awesome and its ability to hold in your mammoth, milky bazookas is the real Christmas miracle here.

"Thanks heaps," you quietly respond.

"So, what's happening with this little... oh. Not so little babe?" she questions, in obvious shock. A WHITECOAT picks up your son's chart and spurts the specky code term for:

"Someone suspects the kid's mother is a dirty whore."

They collectively raise an eyebrow. *Dr H* remains unmoved.

"I don't have a *sinister* and neither does he. We just want the test results so we can go home," you say, deadpan with an eerie emphasis on the dead. *S2* makes her way to your little contamination corner for the first time since you arrived. You suddenly feel very puddly and intimidated and sink into the chair like she's mouthing *"you're dead if you dob."* The situation is that ridiculous.

"It's a suspected... *yadda yadda... my grinchy account is the only worthy one... ignore them,*" she waffles on and even though you comprehend very little of it, you do comprehend the patronising tone.

So does Green Man who steps forward and suddenly seems eight foot tall.

"It's a scraping from the pelvis as he was forcepped out. Surgeon Ninja told me himself it was nothing to worry about and that it would heal. It's a graze, which we've told you a hundred times already. My wife doesn't have a *sinister*. None of us do. I'm sorry, I know it's precautionary, but the whole thing is a joke now. Look at him. Does he look like he should be here?"

The group of officials puff their chests a little as *Dr H* cocks an eyebrow and pulls out her phone. She mumbo's some jumbo, puts the phone back in her pocket and with actual emotion touches the sweet supple skin of your wrinkly rock melon man. She says nothing of the graze, instead picks up his wounded hand and scowls.

"What happened here? Why is he bandaged?"

"Oh, he wriggled when I took his bloods," *S1* crawls out from the outskirts to explain her incompetence with her standard nervous laugh. No one is amused. THE WHITECOATS raise the other eyebrow and *Dr Do-not-pull-that-shit-with-me-H* stares *S1* down to goo. She looks beyond irritated when her phone rings. She "mmm hmm's" a couple of times while looking down at you, gently resting her hand on your shoulder and smiling warmly for the duration of the call. She hangs up and leans down.

"He's clear to go," she announces and you gasp so loudly it sounds as if you've been holding your breath for a thousand years. The tears pour again.

"Thank you! Thank you so much," you blurt manically. Your response is so over the top she looks at you confused, as if you were captives being held against your will. She squats right down, takes both of your hands and looks into your eyes, like she's scraping through all the trauma to get through to sound-of-mind you.

"You are welcome. Make sure you fill out a feedback form and send it in. Okay? Pick one up near reception on your way out," she says, giving you a glowing green light to speak up. It shines as much as her.

"We're just happy we can take our baby home! All our family are waiting to meet him," you gush.

"Of course. Go. Let them enjoy him," *Dr H* says enthusiastically. She pats your shoulder one last time before turning back to her posse.

You take her cue, clearing up as rapidly as your body permits. Green Man gathers Mini-Man and as a trio you finally (and slowly) make your way to the exit. But, the *H-machine* has unfinished business.

"That wound needs to be recorded," she orders the pair then turns her back to leave.

"I think he needs more testing," is (***seriously***) *S2*'s reply. *Dr H* pauses and launches her clap back.

"The results are conclusive. There is nothing more to test. They want to take their child home. It's Christmas."

"We were just following the protocol…"

"Yes, but clearly assumptions were made. Why was that mother so hysterical?"

"She's been like it all week," *S1* shares with a skerrick of guilt, peering sideways at *S2*.

"Mmm," is all *Dr H* says. You want to egg her on to launch an investigation! Hand out some red cards! Give someone a bloody time out! But there is a whole lot of undertone in that *"Mmm"* to appease you… for now. You watch her strut off with THE WHITECOATS flanking her do-not-fCkwith-me aura and fan out a little. You will be forever grateful for the moment she stepped in the room.

You begin your farewells to the staff. You don't particularly like them, but they did care and watch over your child when you were absent. *S1* looks at you suspiciously. You set her at ease and gently pat her arm.

"Thank you. Merry Christmas."

"Thanks, and to you. Enjoy your baby with the fam," she responds sweetly. *S2* interrupts and summons her away. You call out regardless of her never-ending rudeness.

"Merry Christmas." Nothing. You step closer. "Thank you!" Still nothing. You take another step. "Goodbye?" Maybe she didn't hear? She did and ignores you anyway like you officially no longer exist. She even turns her back on what feels like a problem that will not leave. *S1* looks on awkwardly and shrugs her shoulders. Green Man watches on appalled. He grabs your arm and leads you towards the door.

"Forget her," he says at them and ushers you to the exit. "Fuck this place," he says loud enough for everyone to hear and you both walk out for the last time. You can't help but feel an emptiness that an already shitty situation ended in an even shittier way. You will never understand how she developed such intense negatives not only toward a brand new Mum, but to your fresh, innocent babe. You want her to know you really did not mean to cause any trouble. If only she would have dropped her guard for a second you could have told her you understood the pressure she must be under. You would have reassured her you totally got that she was obliged professionally to err on the side of caution for the wellbeing and safety of other patients, parents and staff. But as you say all this to the still seething Green Man he offers a string of truths.

"Why are you making excuses for her? You did nothing wrong and were treated like a leper. The quality of care and support is supposed to extend beyond pregnancy *and* the birth no matter the circumstances. Right? Isn't that what was drilled into you the whole way through this thing? That's what the pamphlets said! There were down times when staff weren't busy and didn't seem under that much pressure and they still treated you like shit. We were an inconvenience they didn't want to deal with. She's just pissed their incompetence was exposed."

"I suppose it would be a hard environment to be empathetic towards adults."

"Bullshit. They were barely empathetic to our son! You didn't deserve any of that. Look at you! You're shaking!"

As you leave the hospital in some sort of confused elation, the three of you huddle out like frightened refugees. It feels like you are escaping an asylum and any moment could be dragged back inside and forced to hand over your baby. It is this frail and toxic frame of mind that goes unchecked for many years. You try to shove it deep down, but it slowly leaks its ugly, undiagnosed-under-the-radar-stock-standard-test-fooling-post-natal trauma all over the next decade. Because you were lucky enough to actually fall pregnant. Because you were fortunate enough to have a healthy child. Because you were privileged to take a healthy baby home at all – who the hell are you to complain compared to so many who have suffered much, much worse? Even if you wanted to the story becomes more and more embarrassing to share as the *sinister* stigma is all people hear when you recall the tale. The guilt, the shame, the emotional baggage is too much to process on top of becoming a new Mum. So you train yourself to shut it away and shut your mouth and pretend it never happened. Eventually, you self-medicate with the heavy-handed help of your soon to be very good pal – Mr Dan Murphy.

You squash this whole ordeal down so well, that after a few years no one – least of all you – realises how much of a head-fCky toll it took. Instead of getting help, you and your brain attempt to erase the awkward, the irritating, the embarrassing, the insulting, the mortifying, the shocking, the betrayal, the angst, the hopelessness, the numbness, the powerlessness, the hurt, the loathing, the sorrow, and all and every bit of pain. Fortunately, you both do a shit job and when you finally give alcohol the flick everything you tried to forget spews across the page in all its raw-as-fCk glory. What starts as self-therapy results in a book's worth of pent up bile.

But not today. Today is the day to finally take your baby home and begin the forgetting.

GO TO: **PAGE 114**

PAGE 54:
CAREER CALAMITY

(from page 92)

Seriously – GET OFF SOCIAL MEDIA! It's anti-health, especially in this state. Being bedridden and alone is not good for your over-thinking mind and you sure are plunging into the depths of topics better left for saner times. The uncertainty of a career and parenting on your own terms are never far from your thoughts. It's becoming a hovering doubt monster over your increasingly tired head. So scrolling through flooded feeds and hashtags with equally nauseating visuals, is dangerous territory. This is the home of highly unrealistic levels of pressure and expectations flying close to an insane sun that spins on an impossibly unachievable axis.

Unfortunately, the pressure to figure out a plan is definitely a real one. You look at your sad little craft corner with its sparkly wooden trinketed Etsy intentions and cry. You've barely been out of the money making game sixteen minutes and you have no idea how to get back in, let alone what the hell to do. Your future wage-earning capabilities are as big a mystery as how you will contribute. Your respect for single Mums sky rockets, as does women in general. How the hell *did they*, *do they* and *will you* pull it all off and still be sane?

You're not looking for quick fix riches, rather flexible solutions.

Your sad bucket list reeks of normality...

-Buying groceries without watching on nervously as you scan your card at the checkout

-Book with abandon the occasional camping trip without calculating the five cent coins scraped off the car floor into the equation

-Hopping on a plane to spend time with family when there are milestones, or funerals without having to take out a loan or sell body parts

-Give to charity without hiding the evidence and feeling like a criminal because you've spent part of the grocery money to do it

-Occasionally buy clothing that won't burn your skin, or shrink if it's humid outside

-Go into a real-life hairdresser and have your witchy locks tended rather than a home colour and cut comprising of you hacking at pigtails with the chicken scissors and finishing with a $9 box job

-Make multiple medical appointments without doing a deal with Rumpelstiltskin

-Date night with dinner AND a movie instead of grappling over which one you can afford and then forget the lot and watch TV in bed with a 99 cent bag of microwave popcorn like you never do every night of the week

The sky falls good and proper on this pity party and you soon give in to a monumentally HUGE panic attack.

DO YOU:
A) SOURCE CHOCOLATE – IT HEALS ALL: PAGE 69
B) BITCH SLAP YOSELF: PAGE 66

PAGE 55:
THE THIRD DAY TIT

(from page 30)

Once upon a time you and your lovely Aunty had the misfortune of being driven to a family event with your sporadically hoofed Mother. To make matters worse, Mum followed her equally lead-footed sister who both insisted on arriving at the destination at warped, erratic speed. Forget facelifts – a force like this shaves years off ageing skin in seconds. Oddly, neither of them broke the law, but their unique execution certainly felt like they should have been imprisoned. You held on for dear life.

"I choose life Mum! I choose liiiiiffffe," you screamed while Aunty got a spinal shunting on a two-wheeled turn and a bonus boob from the repetitive whiplash. She was overjoyed with the upgrade and changed her name to *Three Tittie Tootie*.

Okay... most of that isn't entirely true, but it really has felt like every big breasted relative who ever was – handed the buxom bazoonga baton firmly and largely onto you. But, this current baby boobage predicament is taking the piss and your three titted chest feels more like a rigid panel of wood – not your familiar, pillowy cream-pies.

As soon as the milk is in it apparently wants out and along with it comes a weepy, soppy, irrational version of someone who used to be you. Unlike the poised, alien-looking mothers depicted in your out-of-date baby books – the ***third-day blues*** is a very, very real thing for you and it just sucks arse.

You attempt to feed your orange-skinned jelly boy. The hospital is packed and the only reason you've been here this long is because he looks like a fluro fishing lure. He is one jaundiced cantaloupe and today his eyes are glowing, which seems like some solid proof of your overcooked infant theories – inconveniently ignored by all during the great *INDUCE ME IMMEDIATELY* campaign of last week. But, it's all rather irrelevant now.

The staff have laid him out in his little incubator like a sun baking roast chicken under the rotisserie heat lights. Your tears begin. He wakes up and squawks a little, so you get him out and try a feed. You aren't winning at the breastfeeding thing right now. There are probably five hundred reasons why your bountiful boobies and little red rooster are not nailing it yet, so of course you blame your faulty funbags and if you're going to guilt trip yourself, it might as well be today. Tears drip onto his hungry little lips and make his hair all soggy. The salty taste sends him into a frenzy as he frantically attempts to land his beak on your seething nipple.

"Here it is, little one. You're chomping around like a madman. Take it… please," you plead, but even with his enthusiasm your hungry little plucked peacock will not latch. Your boobs are on fire, your source of release is confused, and you feel like these ridiculous emotions are about to swallow you both at any second. Just as you contemplate thoughts of letting the woe-wave win – a beautiful Midwife enters.

"Come, come now, lovey! It's okay. Stop that crying, sweetheart. Here," she sings and floats in on a cloud of kindness. She hands you a box of tissues and gently helps you with the latching, but chompy chookin is resisting. She covers you up and takes bub.

"Was he crying for a feed, hun?"

"He kind of squawked. I thought I'd try and see if I might have more success than last time."

"Don't mind if he squawks, darl. Wait a little for him to kick up a stink. He'll let you know when he's serious. Until then you rest up and don't worry if everything's not perfect straight away. You'll both get the hang of it soon enough and even if you don't, there's a solution to most problems," says the comforting Midwife. She puts him back into the incubator and pats his bot until he closes his Martian eyes, then makes her way to you – fluffing, fussing, meticulously fixing you and the bed.

"It's just that my boobs are killing. I really don't know what I'm doing," you sob, like a useless failure. Like every bully you ever knew is calling out taunts from the window,

"What was the point of those huge tits if you can't even feed your baby with them!"

The Midwife is having none of it and swoops to the rescue, cape flapping in the breeze. It's Power Pink. Meds kicked in? No. You just need milk relief and now.

"Let's express some of that for you. I'll go get the machine and you dry your eyes and relax. Everything is going to be fine," she reassures soothingly, pats your cheeks with a tissue, and leaves the room. You take a deep breath and are thankful for yet another beautiful soul. You know it's their job, but so many of the staff go way beyond with uncredited kindness and empathy… hang on. Did she just say *machine*? What the holy hell warrants the title *machine* to extract milk from a human? Maybe you misheard.

You did not.

In rolls a contraption that looks like the spaceship that delivered your iridescent, jaundy spawn. It's one Martian too many for you packing your bags.

DO YOU:
A) RELEASE THE BEASTS: PAGE 87
B) RETREAT THE BEASTS: PAGE 112

PAGE 56: THE BIRTH PLAN

(from page 7 & 93)

Ahh the Birth Plan. Thankfully, you have maintained an iota of sanity to realise that writing one does not necessarily equate to how the birth will go. You're a semi-sensible lass who has read enough literature on the cruel realities coming your way. That, and a solid appreciation of never expecting a damned thing in life to run smoothly, plants you firmly into the ground. But, none of this stops you from chalking up a twenty nine page birthy thesis in elaborate script. You wonder what becomes of the magical article afterwards. Do they whip them out when they need a good laugh, or maybe stick on the staff room wall and ditch darts when a patient is not particularly pleasant? They must see some pearlers, though you wonder why pregnant women are encouraged to write out a birth plan at all if it's just going to be ignored. You admit you are adamant about certain things, but are also hyper aware of not pissing off the staff who will bring your baby into the world.

Annoying, silly little parchment or not – it is one of the few things a new Mum-to-be feels like she has any control over and here is where you leave the last kernel of yours:

The Final Birth Plan (draft 1,983ish):

EPIDURAL

Husband, Mother and tag team Aunty in the birth suite

EPIDURAL

NO all-fours. Natural born LUMMOX. Doggy – don't worky. NO interest in the bedroom. NO interest on the birth bed

EPIDURAL

Very ANTI public pooing. PLEASE remove all evidence. I must never know. Ever. There was no poo.

EPIDURAL

The Birth Plan quickly becomes way too much of a reality check of impending pain, gore, awkwardness and poo. Homework was never your thing anyway.

Go have some fun. Time for the baby shower.

GO TO: PAGE 14

PAGE 57:
B) SOBRIETY

(from page 76)

Encouraging a man who has been relatively sober for the majority of his life to now take up heavy drinking – seems irresponsible. Encouraging a man to take up heavy boozing as a coping mechanism for becoming a Father – seems slightly insane. You decide to lure Green Man toward the road of sobriety and invest your efforts into convincing him all will be well and that having a baby truly will be a magical experience – one he will grow to appreciate. You know he'll come around.

Alas, he does not. Years of healthful living and walking the earth like a purpose-driven monk have finally taken their toll. It is nothing short of a miracle he pulled this sober caper off for this long in this country.

On hearing the baby news Green Man takes up drinking like an Olympian and the boys' nights you've been encouraging him to partake in for a decade quickly become messy occurrences. All the disciplined zen is abandoned and what was formerly your husband rapidly morphs into his Green Man namesake with the ever-nearing prospect of becoming a Dad. And what do you do about it? Nothing. Not a damned thing.

Congratulations! You've birthed a boozehound!

You ignore the lot and focus on brewing your bun. Brace yourself. Things are about to get heavy.

GO TO: PAGE 21

PAGE 58:
A CHANGE OF PLANS

(from page 9 & 39)

It all happens so quickly. With every whisper and sideward glance of this new team of infant probing strangers you fight the urge to grab bub and sprint out the door. Before you can, he is whisked away without question. Green Man still hasn't arrived and all you can do is sit on the bed like a rag doll weeping uncontrollably. The angel Midwife looks on baffled by how quickly things have gone from celebration to somewhat mourning. She is soon relieved of her duties and hugs you tightly, still clutching your bags.

"I'm so sorry this has happened to you," she whispers.

"It's okay. Thank you for everything," you whisper back through a wall of tears and watch what feels like your only ally walk out the room. Thankfully, Green Man walks in at the same time and your heart goes out to him. One minute he is taking his little family home – the next he's greeted with a manic wife and no baby to be seen. He frowns and comes to assess you first. You're a mess and barely coherent, but you get a few legible sentences out. He introduces himself to the staff. You don't bother eavesdropping, you just want to leave. Huffing defiantly, you swipe your tears and take a deep breath ready to demand they return your baby and the release papers immediately. You push yourself awkwardly off the bed, but Green Man gets to you first. His expression is strange. You struggle to read it.

"What? What's the matter?"

"They're not sure what the graze is, so they're going to run some tests. They said they're concerned it could be… a *sinister*, but the chances are very low."

"Low for what? A *sinister*?"

"Yeah."

"How? I don't have one. Do you?"

"No. *I* definitely do not," he confidently replies. You note the tone and lock it away in the *things to question later* files. You can't deal with that now. It's hard enough being in this room without screaming.

"Test me," you insist and thrust your bare, desperate arm toward them. "Here! Do it now!"

"That won't be necessary, Mrs Man. We'll monitor Master Man and run a few tests, anyway. Pre-cautionary…" The random doctor you have just met tries to defuse your eager veins.

"But, I don't…"

"Don't worry, Mrs Man. You'll most likely have him home for Christmas. It's better to be safe than sorry," he cuts you off and before you can tell him to shove his patronising clichés up a nostril, you are advised to stay in the room (one that some poor Mum is probably desperate to get into) and await further instructions.

They leave you alone. Without the crib. Without your baby who is who knows where, far away from where he should be going. Home. With his parents. Now. Your legs seem to melt and you barely land on the edge of the bed. Green Man consoles you best he can, but even he is in shock by what just transpired. You cry and you cry and you cry some more. You try to pull yourself together, but the more you try the more hysterical you become. It seems to take forever and Green Man is completely out of his capability zone. You want to reassure him you'll be fine. You want to put your usual optimistic spin on things and polish the proverbial turd. But this thing is unpolishable and the sorrow infests you like mould. Seconds ago your baby was by your side – now he is not and deep down in the intuitive sub-cockles a psychic something whispers of worse things to come.

Green Man watches on hopelessly and begins pacing. He belts out a string of profanities to the air, kisses you on the forehead and reassures you he'll be back. You don't even notice he's gone. You've made yourself a little canyon and have crawled into it. You hover in that lifeless hole for what seems like an eternity, until Green Man throws the door open with the angel Midwife in tow.

"Oh, sweet girl! Come on. Let's fix you up. You've got yourself into a state again!"

"Is he okay?"

"Of course. They've taken the tests already."

"This is so horrible. I don't have a *sinister*," you whisper.

"It's just a precaution."

"Yes, but you've seen him all week. You know he scraped my pelvis."

"I know. They just want to be sure."

"Can I see him?"

"Yes. Let's pack you up and I'll take you to him."

"Can I take him home?"

"I'm not sure, lovey. The staff will take care of you. They'll let you know everything," she says and offers you a wheelchair you stupidly decline. Green Man picks up the bags and you both slowly follow the angel down to a place you will come to loathe. A place designed to save sweet, innocent infants and reassure weary parents. A place that will become one of judgement and embarrassment. A place where you and your baby are made to feel unwelcome and unclean.

GO TO: **PAGE 38**

PAGE 59: BESTIE TO THE RESCUE

(from page 34)

Bestie walks in and the tears you had managed to sort of contain flood uncontrollably again. She waves her wand and removes all the bad vibes in the room. It takes this angel merely seconds to realise the issues afoot. She scans the room, surveys the damage, checks bub is in good hands and flies over to you. She's just a beautiful snuggly blanket of warmth and love and you feel like a child safely tucked up in bed – where no harm will come while she is near. You look at each other without words and immediately know the other's thoughts. She gives the bosses the nod to take their leave and their brief visit is done.

"Third day sucks, hey. He's so beautiful by the way."

"He looks like he's from planet banana."

"He looks perfect, and he's awesome," she says lovingly and you nod, tears still leaking. Bestie detaches the machine, pushes it far away and covers you up. She retrieves your bra knowing it's your dying wish to be buried with one on and correctly presumes post childbirth would be no different. She moves around the room between you and bub, blessing you with her selflessness and showing more compassion and care in a few seconds than you were denied by a trained professional only moments before. Bestie gave birth a mere two months ago and yet here she is doting.

She brings out her stashed smorgasbord of pate, soft cheeses and every cured meat ever made and apologises about a soft serve that melted in the car. You adore her for everything and blubber some more. As she hands you some tissues one of her breast pads pops out onto your face and you both piss yourselves laughing. There is no medicine more powerful than a soul sister whose stupid is as silly as your own. She is the best anti-depressant and just a spoonful of Bestie makes the bullshit sod right off for a few precious moments. You wish you could bottle her for everyone to have a taste of her sunshiny goodness... in the most well-meaning and non-cannibalistic way.

Your original Midwife comes back in the room and Bestie informs her of everything. She rips into the *midwitch* and the hospital for allowing someone like that to exist on a maternity ward. Even more magical than her mood-changing qualities – Bestie has a unique ability to *have-a-gripe* in such a way that by the end of it the two of them are blissfully swapping cocktail recipes and re-writing Midwifery policies. It's a unique gift. She's a keeper.

After all this you just want to go home. Problem is bub is still a bit too *sunset orangey* and you are yet to release the mandatory number 2, let alone crack the code on breastfeeding. They convince you to stay one more night on the proviso that pending bubs fluorescence, and your bowel emptying – you can be home before Christmas. You grab the meal form and order prune juice with eggs extra oily and a side order of butter that you neck like a *slippery nipple* shooter. That thing is coming out by hook or by crook.

Time to get out of here. Time to get your baby out of here. Time to get a skerrick of control back over your body and begin your Mum life. Time to go home.

GO TO: PAGE 9

PAGE 60:
A) WAIT FOR ASSISTANCE

(from page 2)

You decide to wait a bit longer. Surely someone will come in soon. If not to check on you – at least on bub. You had your baby in the late afternoon and it's been a few hours since. There is a bit of commotion on the ward. Lots of babies crying and it sounds like every button in the hospital is buzzing. You don't want to add to the drama. Bub still sleeps and the pain is manageable. It is a bit gross lying in a blood pool, but nothing you can't deal with. You stare at your little miracle who sleeps soundly, as you too go in and out of consciousness. Finally, someone puts their head through the doorway.

"Okay. Now where are we at… Mrs…?" a Midwife questions loudly. She's talking to the clipboard, not you – an act you'll grow so accustomed to you won't bother acknowledging some of them back in a few days.

"Man," you answer, eager to see her.

"Right. Everything okay? Yes. Okay. Someone will be in to sort you out soon," she tells the clipboard then runs to leave the room.

"Um… sorry, but when can I have a shower? I'm still…"

"The anaesthetic hasn't completely worn off yet, so we'll give it a bit longer. Someone will be in soon. Just sit tight."

"Oh... okay..." you quietly respond, but she's gone. Back to waiting and looking at bub who you awkwardly pull into your arms and snuggle tight, despite all the tubes still attached. You cross your fingers he doesn't want a feed while no one is available to help. Luckily he just gurgles and sleeps contently against your warmth that soon disappears.

Hours go by. The madness of the ward does not wane and the pain of your wounds, along with the birthing aftermath, have arrived in full force. The blood has soaked completely through the top sheet and you wouldn't be surprised if it's dripping onto the floor. Thankfully, there is a thin hospital blanket you pull over yourself. You have been wheeled it seems directly under a vent and the combination of the cold blood and air conditioning has a popsicle effect. Usually, you are the world's biggest sweater and have always made it your mission to locate the air con whenever out and about. The irony is not lost, but you are too cold to care. You have rung the buzzer twice, and no one has come. You don't want to be a bother, but you are shivering and it's after midnight now. So you press the buzzer again and nervously wait. The last thing you want to do is piss off a bunch of stressed-out staff.

GO TO: PAGE 97

PAGE 61:
B) DISTRACTIONS

(from page 72)

You are officially a dysfunctional soup of depressive, uncontrollable emotions and wayward hormones. Your sanity reserves are close to depletion and the uncertainty of how long you can bottle the lot up is unnerving. So you reluctantly try to keep busy. All your body will allow physically are interactions from the chair. You help your Mum untangle the four billion trinkety decorations she's brought from her personal stash and raise an unfestive brow. She ignores it and gives you a big kiss on the cheek leaving you to unravel the ravel.

It reminds you of Chrissy comedies and for the first time in a long time you laugh out loud. You can't wait to share all your faves with your children and hope they will have the same obscure sense of humour handed down by your father (apparently the very unfunny dust bowl of outback Australia drew out the hilarity gene of your ancestors and you are gifted the family *haha* trait). You reminisce of the bond the two of you forged. When most girls were watching Care Bear cartoons, you were cacking yourself at every inappropriate comedy not-meant-for-the-viewing-of-children.

A phone call from your Dad is just the medicine you need:

DAD: How ya goin?

YOU: I'll be right.

DAD: Yeah, well, take it easy.

YOU: I am. I'm untangling lights.

DAD: Righto. Wanna talk about it?

YOU: The lights?

DAD: No, you dill.

YOU: Nup.

DAD: Well, ring me if you need to.

YOU: Thanks, Dad. I will.

DAD: Yeah, alright. By the way, for Christmas lunch I'm bringin' a prawn platter, coleslaw, potato salad, garden salad, bread rolls, a ditty plate and I made a plum pud, but I'm just buyin the shop stuff this year…"

He trails off for forty eight minutes about the trials and tribulations of brandy custard and then takes you on a mental mystery tour of all the thoughts he's been holding onto for the last month. Before you know it you're a full bottle on Australian politics; American politics; the Pakistani cricket team; salmonella; the rugby grand final; the AFL grand final; Viking cheese; an update on his swimming pool frog friends he managed not to murder with chlorine this year, a mandatory Navy story from his glory days and a quick tale about a thrashing he once got from his brothers when he trashed their new bike. You've heard it at least a dozen times. It's still funny. No interaction with your Father is complete without reference to his childhood, which as he pushes on in age you appreciate more and more. After a lifetime of poo-pooing your Dad and his often long-winded nattering – you couldn't be more grateful for his random insights on the world right now. You both know his waffling is purposeful and you love him for it.

DAD: ... yeah so I called the plumber and you don't even wanna know what that bastard charged me *just* to have a look! Well. You'll be right. Plenty of women in our family did it tough and came through, love.

YOU: Probably all that Viking cheese.

DAD: We could be part Viking you know.

YOU: It would explain a lot.

DAD: Sure would. Righto. I'm off. Seeya Sundie. Take it easy. Luv ya.

And bang – he hangs up. The man might waffle for nineteen hours straight, but he is KING of efficient exits. No mucking about.

As visions of those wonderful memories dance about you realise his phone call worked a treat and yay, you have finished untangling the lights. You smile contently in a happy space and for the briefest moment are unbothered by the only element missing – your child.

Your sore body soon betrays the peace with a mandatory loo run and you make the mistake of going past the nursery. The house of comedy cards and distractions come crashing down and you are right back in your dark canyon once more.

You tried. It didn't work. You're over it.

Back to the hospital to demand your child.

GO TO: PAGE 75

PAGE 62: SEX

(from page 37)

Sex is interesting when you're pregnant. Your wayward hormones have you either loathing all things dangling OR sending sexy texties demanding Green Man come home to service your undercarriage at 12:30 in the afternoon. It's quite the contrasting conundrum. Problem is his work place is so far away that by the time he gets home – jeans near his ankles, tripping over lusty limbs – you've either switched back to loathe mode, or moved on. Usually to food. It's a cruel whip lashing you really have no control over.

GM: Ready?

YOU: Meh.

GM: Ay? But you rang me! FOR SEX!

YOU: I know and I really am sorry!

GM: You wanted it an hour ago.

YOU: Yes, but now I want a chip sandwich and a nap. I can't control it.

GM: But it's yoni time. You were gonna getcha yoni on.

YOU: I'm sorry babe. We're gonna have to put a pause on the yonnying.

GM: Boo. What am I 'sposed to do with this?

YOU: I'm choosing not to answer, or look at that.

GM: I'll be in the shower.

YOU: Of course you will.

GM: Shit is blue! It's damaging to toy with a man like this.

YOU: I'm sure you'll be fine. You wanna chip sammich? Salt and vinegar.

GM: Pass.

Poor Green Man. It's a miracle he doesn't put his neck out with all that head shaking. His life has become one long wheel of misfortune and every moment is a commiseration for his mojo:

BAD L_CK BUDDY

BETTER L_CK NEXT T_ME

BACK TO _ORN

Luckily, a few hours later he has a win and it's yay for yoni time. You take a wide birth with your wider girth down the hall in what you think is a seductive swagger. It's really not and you nearly knock him out trying to do *sexy*. He couldn't give three shits – he just wants in. This somewhat odd and very unco display continues in the bed as position after position is attempted like a really disturbing match of limby twister. You used to be so bendy and pliable, but with a gutful of baby interrupting everything – sex is just a complicated mess and you have to frequently pause to catch your breath from all the effort.

You both finally find some version of a sweet spot and everyone is eventually satisfied – if not a little scarred by the ordeal. You look over at Green Man who is smiling. Mint. Harmony at last.

Sex is exhausting work, so you waddle off to the kitchen and neck half a bottle of *Lik-Wid-Choc* and a couple of pieces of peanut butter, banana, lettuce and honey on toast. Go for it. No one but your butt is judging and you got plenty of lycra to rectify the rapidly expanding rectal region.

While you graze away, it's time to contemplate preparations for party season.

GO TO: PAGE 31

PAGE 63:
B) SLEEP IT OFF

(from page 14)

Leave it for tomorrow. You'll be fine. Right? Wrong. Again. It's tomorrow. You are far from fine. You did too much. You are absolutely fCked. Like seriously? What a moron. Once you unwrapped the four billion decorations, you realised the majority of them needed to be hung from the ceiling. This would have been fine had you a step ladder to sticky tape all the sparkle-darkles from the roof. Alas, you don't own a step ladder. So, like a poorly balancing hippopotamus you somehow climbed and contorted yourself onto a wafer thin bar stool at least a hundred times. Up and down like a really, really bad circus act – the kind disgruntled patrons throw rotten vegetables at. What started out semi-simple eventually became laboriously slow and painful. The only sturdy element of this plan was the craftsmanship of the stool. You consider last night's goat curry as an offering to the Swedish furniture gods and forget it seventeen seconds later. Not only did you overdo the decorating, but you underestimated how much preparation needed to be done. Cleaning, vacuuming, baking, maneuvering furniture and a myriad of totally ridiculous chores that a woman of your size and stage of pregnancy probably shouldn't have entertained.

You didn't ring anyone for help and now you've awoken to find you can barely move. You know you've pushed yourself way too far and along with the usual pains there are a few new ones. Panic sets in and concerns for the baby outweigh all. You ring the hospital and they recommend you come in, which you do with your tail between your swollen legs.

GO TO: PAGE 42

PAGE 64:
B) KEEP WAFFLING

(from page 84)

After rabbiting on about baby names, hospitals and way too much vagina talk there is an eerie silence on the other end of the phone. Suddenly, one of his work colleagues comes on the line.

"Hey. You better come get G-Man. He's staring blankly and not speaking. It's freaking the customers out," he says. Well done. It has barely started and you've already broken the reluctant Father-to-be. You decide to hold off on another onslaught of embryo enthusiasm and pat his leg sympathetically.

Once home a sudden surge of unexplainable-untamable-irritation comes over you. You tighten your hold and pull Green Man close to your seething lips.

"I love you, but you better hurry up and get a grip because *this* is happening," you whisper icily and drift inside like something from a horror film. He shudders.

Yes – you appreciate everyone has a breaking point, but unfortunately for Green Man he is about to learn that his breaking point is as useful as a soggy old piece of lettuce. With the catastrophic baby crap storm that's coming, he'll need to build some breaking point muscle ASAP!

He fires up the laptop and purchases some additions for the home gym. Not quite the literal 'muscle' metaphor you were suggesting, but it's a start.

On a separate note – let's give a round of applause to our newest pregnant member to the *Society of the Hormonally Unstable.*

Welcome aboard loopo.

RETURN TO: PAGE 10

PAGE 65:
B) CUE BESTIE

(from page 33)

You and Bestie have not only just gone through the wedding journey, but are now pregnant together too. While neither of you admits it publically, you were secretly in cahoots to fall around the same time and lo-and-behold your borderline weirdo plans came to fruition. What looked like a healthy, slightly obsessive friendship was actually a masterminded plot all along. She bought a house – then you bought a house. She got engaged – then you got engaged. She got married – then donned a managerial hat and set to your nuptials prep like a woman possessed. Wedding planners be damned! This chick was a wedding ninja who channelled your tastes into tangible realities and even put having her own child on hold until your wedding was over! Driven by an insane determination that your babies would be bestest buds come hell or broken waters. That – and she secretly wanted to get guilt-free shitfaced with you on your special day.

Every damned day of this friendship you have wondered when it will all be over, because putting it mildly – you have never deserved this girl. The bond was solidified very early on when she whipped you up a batch of cake batter after a big, boozy night out. You sat on the kitchen floor like mischievous eight year olds, giggling hysterically with beaters and bowls and wooden spoons while blobs of delicious, raw chocolate surprise dripped down your chins. What soul wouldn't want to attach itself to that level of deliciousness?

She is an angel and in a perfect, copyright/trademark-free world you would list all the famous partnerships there ever was and compare their loveliness to her. Alas, you can barely afford an editor, let alone a lawyer, so you throw out a blanket statement – that ***she*** is the epitome of what a best friend should be.

For whatever reason she always believes in and champions you. Bestie is all that is good and light and love in this world and you are like a soggy old sausage in a mud puddle compared to her grace. It would take at least five full lifetimes to repay everything she so selflessly does and probably longer with your useless inability of repaying that level of giving. She sees something in you that most don't and you truly and absolutely love her. Taco is not really your preferred meal choice – especially if a nice bratwurst or cacciatore is on offer, but you could be open to switching menus for her if she wanted. Regardless of throbbing cured meats and Mexican food – you would happily grow old with Bestie. You vow one day you'll write a ridiculous book and tell her she is actually your soul mate. You will reassure her Green Man is totally fine with it and has developed an immunity to your blatant favouritism. He kind of always knew anyway and finds the whole salsa/sausage thing arousing as only his mind would.

Exhibit A: Bestie's Selfless Madness Flashback:

Moments after Bestie gives birth she not only takes your call, but wants to make sure you are okay! FROM THE BIRTHING BED! Still covered in bloody slime and shlop. Just to clarify – she insists on taking the phone to makes sure that your non-pummelled, unbirthy self is fine.

Feeling wretched? You are, but don't worry – you eventually come through for her and her milky tits, which you can reminisce in the third trimester. For now it's time to find out the sex of this bub and Bestie is your honorary husband today.

Guzzle those fluids and hold onto that piss. Time to find out if you're packing a teeny tiny set of gnarly nurries, or omnificent ovaries.

GO TO: PAGE 4

PAGE 66:
B) BITCH SLAP YO SELF

(from page 54 & 69)

Thankfully, you remember what an extraordinarily awesome life you lead, that you have everything you need to pay the bills and even though Green Man is one with the clouds right now, he is not abandoning anyone any time soon. So, calm your frayed self down. The world is not coming to an end – you are having a baby.

You remind yourself not to compare you, your body, your capabilities, your path, your journey, your children, your marriage, your family, your life to anyone else's. It just leads to a shit show of stupidity and time wasting. Time that could be spent servicing your soul, or more importantly – eating. So you let it all go. You delete the social media apps, download pregnancy trackers and the only books you read are Mum & Bub ones, or sci-fi fantasy about hot steamy elves. You want your baby to grow up in a toxic-free space and it starts here – gifting your mind an escape from all the noisy ridiculousness of the world.

All this culling feels great and good news – the *glow* is in. You radiate. It's a beautiful, chilly spring day, so you set up a disintegrating camp chair outside in the sun, slap on your favourite daggy baggies and grab those books. You read. You bask. You pick flowers and make the daisy chains you did as a little girl, weaving them into your hair. You feel pretty and grateful. You rub your belly endlessly. You do absolutely nothing else but think of holding bub in your arms. You feel the most divine flood of love and warmth overcome you – like your baby can hear and feel it all. You suddenly feel very grounded. It's magical.

Bring on the final show. You are ready.

TIME FOR THE THIRD TRIMESTER

GO TO: PAGE 50

PAGE 67:
IT IS TIME TO GO

(from page 91)

You feel a warm rush of liquid and make your way to the toilet. Holy moly it's happening! Unsure what to do, you strip off and re-dress in another tent nightie, then shove a few flannels into a fresh pair of knickers. You prepared for everything apart from goo catchment. You wait for fear to kick in. It doesn't. You suddenly feel as warm as the goo and eerily elated. You must tell dearest Green Man the news. Off you pop. It feels like you could be skipping, in fact you're pretty sure you are. You tenderly stroke the alcohol-laden film of sweat from his clammy arm.

"Babe. Babe… it's happening…" you whisper softly. He grunts and rolls over into his doona cocoon. You are fully aware you are prodding a slumbering wildebeest, but probe on anyway.

"Babe. Babe… the baby... it's coming! Wake up…"

"Fuuuuucckkk ooooooouuuuugggghhhhhhffffffffffffffffffff!!!" groans the drunken, hideous mess that was formerly your husband. He has transformed into a crazed, furless blanket monster. The doona appears to be a part of him – a large coat hiding a growth, like a mammoth pimple of procrastination and it has just burst its heinous puss of reality all over Green Man's denial parade. He channels the cries of a wounded sabre tooth and goes back to sleep. You manically giggle. You are too deep in pixelated pixie world right now to care.

"Okay. You rest a bit longer. But, you should probably have a shower because we may have to leave soon," you sing and glide out in a heavenly mist knowing your response to such vileness is especially abnormal for minimal vile tolerance you. This baby really is coming.

At the other end of the house, Mum has taken up residency in preparation for the arrival of her grandbaby. Having her around is wonderful, and she has really relished her return to *Mumma-mode* after sitting on the sidelines of your life for the last few decades. An impressive feat considering she was most definitely not designed for sideline sitting in any form.

MUM IDOL FLASHBACK

There is a grainy photo of you and your Mum at a balmy family shindig. It's not the greatest picture of either of you, nor is it posed, but it's one of your faves. You are a toddler looking up at her, waffling about something – and she looks down at you with an expression epitomising motherly love.

Your Mum was always a celebrity in your eyes and those hazy early childhood memories were filled with awe and observation. A champion in sports and life she has always been someone everyone wants to be around. A draw card in the crowd, valued and respected. Hers is a work ethic equalled by few and it is a monumental shame more of that steel focus and determination didn't filter into you. She had no need for bra-burning. Her power was strategically subtle. On the civilian front – a commanding regal grace. On the court – a no nonsense warrior. There was no greater super heroine for a little girl. That grainy photo not only captured the adoration of a child for her mother, but the essence of her greatest skill set and achievement – pure, unconditional and beautiful "Mumming."

Charming, darling idol flashbacks aside – up until this point it's been less about reflective mother/daughter worshipping and more about baby candy bling. She's been pushing you to breed for years and is loving every second that brings her closer to mauling her grandson with lipsticky kisses the minute he shoots out. Nonna is gonna wear that baby like a pair of Gucci sunnies. As far as all the "warrior-woman-walking-the-earth-like-a-moral-compass-with-legs" talk goes – that regal crown slips slightly this night. She too enjoyed the evening's frivolity, indulging in a little tipple herself (though would spend the next decade pleading her innocence).

It's just after midnight, so of course she's casually chatting on the phone like it's five in the afternoon. In her defence it is her husband on the other end.

"Mum, my waters broke."

"Hang on, love," she continues, obliviously. You giggle.

"Mum. It's happening."

"Just a minute, love…" she calls again and puts the *hold-on* finger up and still you chuckle.

"Hey! Mum! My waters broke!"

"Ay? Oh shit! Right. How exciting! Hang on. Yeah… her waters have broken," she actually pauses to update the recipient, putting him on hold and even then *still* does not hang up. "Have you rung the hospital, love? Go and ring them and I'll finish up here and get ready."

"Okay," you gaily respond and off you flutter like a demented woodland fairy to ring the hospital without question. Whoever you speak to is far more accommodating than your limp support unit. She helps you count the contractions and recommends you make your way in.

"Is there someone there to drive you, dear?"

"................. Yep. Sure is," you lie, badly. She gives you a string of information you hope isn't important because you have no recollection of a thing she said after you hang up.

"What did she say, love?" your Mum calls out from the bathroom. She's just having a quick shower to freshen up like you're all just popping down the local shops to get milk, or partaking in some other non-waterbreaky activity.

"Ummm... not to panic and to start making our way in."

"Was that all?" she questions, knowingly. This Woman has seen and heard a lifetime of your vagueness and intuitively knows something is up. She blames a lack of concentration. You blame being in utero during a championship match and a few celebratory after game vodkas. No wonder you're shit at math's, memory recall and anything requiring fine motor skills.

"Ummmmm... oh.... yeah.... she just wanted to know if someone could drive."

"Well, I suppose I could..."

"I'm fine to drive, Mum."

"Are you sure?"

"Yes..." you answer, not sure at all as another contraction presents itself.

"Mmm. I don't know. Clearly *he* can't. Where is he anyway?"

The shower is suddenly running and by some miracle Green Man is up. You speaking sweetly was the defibrillating jolt he needed. *Normal* you has been very direct of late, sugar coating nothing. But not tonight. In your mind you are one of the ballerinas from the Nutcracker and considering what's to come – you will wish you clawed tighter to that flittery, sugar-plum fairy delusion.

DO YOU:
A) WHO WILL DRIVE: PAGE 5
B) CATCH A TAXI: PAGE 103

PAGE 68:
THE BABY EXPO

(from page 4 & 20)

Y ou and Bestie go to your first ever baby convention with starry eyes and pockets full of cash you stupidly think will be enough. Rookies. It's never enough. There is an insatiable baby shopping beast that you will undoubtedly feed until the end of time. It is never truly satisfied. There will always be something else that you, or your child apparently *needs*.

BARELY AN HOUR LATER...

The two of you roll out like stuffed jalapeno poppers – overheated and sucked dry. You stand outside shallow breathing, still in shock at what you just witnessed. Bellies. Bellies everywhere. Soooo many bellies.

BARELY AN HOUR BEFORE...

You may have peaked a little too soon with your **eXpo** enthusiasm, but at least you got it out of your systems while you can still see your toes. It's a shame this was your first initiation into the world of commercial motherhood. You guys are at the *just-got-over-morning-sickness-naively-excited-baby-land* stage. Translation = two limbed lollipops. Walking suckers welcoming every con artist into your hearts and wallets and happily so because you're *First Time Mummies!* and prepared to have the piss pulled.

But, you were not prepared for this and it bitch slaps you both on entry in all its maternal glory. The graphic realities of pregnancy and birth are a bit of a shock to the uninitiated and especially you who (still on chapter one of the few baby books you own) are in a bit of a baby denial bubble. So casual chatter of breast leakage, nipple cracking and any reason that would possess you to buy an arse cushion – is a bit of a confronting wake-up call. You know disturbing things are on the horizon, but you're happy ignoring them for now. Foreign concepts like *expressing* and accompanying ten-foot posters displaying the act – are downright horrifying. Seriously. What is going on here? What happened to the whole boob-baby-mouth-rainbows and earth-goddess images you conjured in your mind? Why would you want to shove those demonic suckers to your tits on purpose? You're still processing the whole watermelon squeezing out a pea-hole stage and frankly don't need these additional freak-outs just yet. You both look a bit queasy and what's worse, this is just the entrance! You're out of your depth.

Further along stalls are squashed in like a downtown fish market where everyone yells out their wares, or shoves them into your faces as woman after woman pushes through to sign up or clean up. It is the most surreal spectacle and you and Bestie are quietly horrified. Even though the comically labelled "*$how $pecial$*" are so mortifyingly overpriced – people line up in droves to get their piece of the baby pie. It's like the end of the world, but instead of clawing to get pallets of water – these impregnated zombies are belly bumping each other for muck mats and bath time jugs. The only sane refuge is a community stall offering info on local services like Mothers groups, Health Nurses and library activities for Mums and bubs. You have a brief chat to a kindly spoken volunteer until she makes the mistake of eagerly passing you an information bag and then the vultures descend.

"We've only got a few! We've only got a fewwwwwww!!" the poor woman yells at the crowd, but her cries are soon muffled. You both watch on helplessly as the swarm engulf her like locusts, pushing you and Bestie to the outskirts again. Shuffled by the masses, you are moved along the aisles that never seem to end. Finally, in the distance you see an exit near the food hall.

What's it going to be?

DO YOU:
A) GO TO THE FOOD HALL: PAGE 27
B) SPRINT TO THE EXIT: PAGE 109

PAGE 69:
A) SOURCE CHOCOLATE

(from page 54)

YES. Chocolate is **ALWAYS** the answer.

Unfortunately, after you recover from the cacao-coma, you still wallow in your deeply dug comparison-hole. Head back for some well needed therapeutic bitch-slapping.

GO TO: PAGE 66

PAGE 70:
BABY GIRL IS COMING

(from page 94)

This is like a damned hotel. It's a dream. You are induced. There is definite discomfort and pain, but nothing compared to the horror stories you've heard. You are coping nicely. Everything about this experience is nice. Super nice. There is an actual waiting suite that looks like a lounge room. You look over at your family and ponder the miracle of life and this amazing moment they are privy to witness from the comfort of cushy couches. Green Man watches wrestling highlights on his phone while your Mum rides her addiction wave of *Lolly-Squash* on hers. You just got her signature 'hang-on-a-minute-love' finger, mid-contraction. She is about to conquer the highest level and is unfortunately out of lives. The miracle of life may truly be a huge feat, but with the hours that woman has put into that game – this really is a big moment.

Unbothered, you reach for the remaining ice chip and suck away contently. A few hours later your baby girl is born. Ta daa! She is perfect and reminds you of a bumbalina doll, which reminds you of some of your favourite comedy Queens[4] and you start cacking

---

[4] *Kath & Kim: Written by Gina Riley, Jane Turner, Magda Szubanski*

yourself on the birth bed. It's a sign your name choice is clearly aligned with the stars.

Bumbalina Bonzai Scarlett Slay Man.

It's perfect. At least it sounds perfect to you – though everyone in the room including Green Man, your Mother, the obstetrician, at least six midwives, a cleaner, some guests that aren't even yours and a random priest gently inform you of the seventy one day grace period (most likely invented for munted Mummies in a poor-decision-making fog) to think it over and maybe reconsider. You ignore them all and proudly mark it onto the purple info book thingy that you will lose at least a hundred and fifty times over the next five years. That bastard will **never** be where it should be when you need it.

On your final checkup (and in a voice slightly livelier than his usual mono tone) the wonderful obstetrician happily agrees to deliver your next child. Apparently it's a bit of a big deal to be blessed with this offer by this particular professional and you, in typical clueless fashion, are oblivious. *Dr Vanilla* is quite the sought after womb-servicer and it was a miracle he *chose* you at all. His is a reputation of exclusively favouring industry clientele and rarely engaging with the honey pots of the general public. You, being the antithesis of exclusivity and as general as they come – are honoured by the return invitation and spotlight on your average, yet stellar pregnancy game. It has you puffy. You puff up a storm. It's a foreign feeling. You were never worthy, nor motivated enough for awards and being told you're essentially a *low maintenance birther* – is as good as a trophy. In fact, you ponder a little bronze vagina up on the shelf and imagine the ice breaking potential that doozy could have during the many play-dates you will spend most of your kids' childhoods trying to get out of.

Many years later you and Green Man attend a school assembly for your son. Student after student receive accolades for greatness in academic and sporting achievements. Then it's Mini-Man's turn. Green Man fires up the zoom lens and you both await the big moment. What's it gonna be? Math's? Writing? Science? Relay? No. Not this kid. His merit certificate trumps all:

AWARDED TO MASTER MAN: FOR BEING A GREAT KING

Why, of course. He is after all –

SON OF THE GREAT BIRTHER & HER ROYAL AVERAGE UTERUS

Bow down bishes.

Righto – moving on before your crazy head gets too big for your crazy crown. This moment is for your lovely little Missy.

GO TO: PAGE 49

PAGE 71:
A) BEERPALOOZA

(from page 76)

You suggest a nice drive to a local brewery and Green Man happily agrees. He orders a share plate with every conceivable soft bloody cheese and cured meat ever fermented. So many favourites and somehow you find the strength not to hurl the plate through the air in a cacciatore friz-*bree* frenzy. Way to maintain control. Green Man takes a moment to draw breath from his food inhalement and looks over at you.

"Why aren't you eating?"

"I'm not hungry," you unconvincingly reply.

"Why aren't you drinking?"

"I'm not in the mood."

"Why are your big ole eyes staring at my beer and the platter then?"

"What is this? Question time with bearded riding hood?" you snap.

This is not going to plan. You hardly blame his suspicions. Up until this point your husband has no idea who you are without a wine in your hand. Goon is so firmly attached to your identity it's like an extra limb. This drinkless version of his wife is virtually a stranger, so of course he's going to be wary of sober you.

"What's wrong? Are you sick?"

"No. Yes. Sort of. Drink your beer," you insist, thrusting the foaming glass forward. He downs it without question and you order another.

"Na, I'm good," he declines and reaches over, almost slipping off the sweat-fest of your newfound clamminess.

"Hold that thought," you insist and slap some money on the bar.

"What's going on with you? Even your skin is acting weird."

"I have some news," you share with a voice that even weirds you out. A sudden freeze comes over his face and you are quietly impressed at his perception – whether he knows what's coming or not. You stall.

"Wanna guess?"

"Not if it's what I think it is," Green Man offers through a gob of teeth grit. Thankfully, the bartender slaps a cold, crafty stout right in front of him and he slugs a hearty gulp. You wait until he draws breath then drop your infant bomb.

"We're going to have a baby. You can skull now," you say, which he does – the entire glass then embraces you.

"Alright then. Baby, hey? Cool. You're going to be a Mum! And I'm going to be a Dad. Well… fCk me. Awesome. I'm going to need another beer."

"You do that," you agree heartily chalking it up for the win. He drinks three more pints, spews twice on the side of the freeway before you arrive home and drag him into bed. You soon learn this will become a common occurrence over the next nine months, though **nothing** compared to the grand finale. For now you don't care. Green Man needs to know he is going to be a Father and you need him to occasionally hold a bucket when it's your turn to spew.

Get the show on the road.

GO TO: PAGE 21

PAGE 72:
NO HOMECOMING FOR BABY

(from page 19 & 74)

You are still in pain. But you sit. Silent. Numb. Babyless. In the same spot you had sat a few months ago, watching trick or treaters, channeling Mila Kunis before she lost her shit and turned green. You eagerly awaited a knock on the door, instead little ghosts and fairies skipped past the house thinking no one was home. Green Man arrived to his heavily pregnant wife rocking near the window, dripping tears into an uneaten cauldron of candy corn and jelly eyeballs.

"Poor witchy-poo. C'mon, I'll eat your reject lollies," he had sweetly soothed and gleefully gorged the lot.

Today you barely rock. You may not be wearing the costume, but you are channelling some very Halloweeny vibes.

At least my baby was with me then, you vent to yourself. Poor me/sad sack bitterness is tricky to navigate in witch-mode. A few centuries before you would have been burned at the stake, or at the very least committed. You truly look like a deranged ghoul. Everything about you is dark and ominous. Your clothing, your eyes, your stringy, unwashed hair that falls across your mopey, disgruntled face – just as it had in your late teens. The pain is as dark as that era too, like a toxic scream it slashes and rips at your insides trying to claw to the sallow surface. It desperately wants to escape, but you forbid it. So it thrashes and protests like a crazed prisoner, while you sit silently in pain – numb and babyless, ignoring it.

The world bustles about unsure how to deal with you. An empty crib and no baby to nurse deserves a rather anti-homecoming queen and you honour her in all your filterless majesty. A big family Christmas gathering is the furthest thing from your mind, but it rolls ever closer in its tinsel-draped-champagne-fuelled-pork-crackling glory. Everyone scurries around in preparation for family festivities and the arrival of a Christmas baby, while a festering chunk of you sits silently loathing it all.

You and Green Man continue to go back and forth to the hospital as often as you can insist without appearing manic. Every day you ask when they will release your babe and desperately plead your innocence. But the test results have still not returned and you both walk out childless, powerless and embarrassed. This was not part of the plan and you know there are a million cases far worse and worthier of pining about than yours. The etching guilt takes its toll. You had prepared for many scenarios including the most tragic ones leading up to, during and after giving birth, but in none of these hypothetical disasters did you counter in *misdiagnoses*. The angst is gross and you feel despicable that any of it is real.

Your family make light of the situation with distractions and well-meaning pep talks, but you are here for none of it. The worried exchanges increase, so you feign a few smiles to avoid looking suicidal, which thankfully you are not. But, your ability to dilute the truth is minimal right now. Your baby is motherless, no one has a clue when he'll be home and frankly, you can't be arsed hiding the emptiness that consumes you. You are openly gutted, unapologetically flayed and the rawest you have ever allowed others to see. You get how alarming it must seem. Your mask has talent. Very few, if any, have seen you as dark and down as this, though you've been here plenty of times before – crouched on shower floors, weeping silently into pillows, driving down long, isolated roads losing it, but *never* with an audience. Today you hide nothing and those normally shielded have front row seats to this sad, hopeless, foreign version of seemingly always sunny you. That *you* would be mortified by your behaviour. This *you* feels nothing. Neither *you* has control over any of it.

DO YOU:
A) DISTRACTIONS: PAGE 61
B) BACK TO BUB: PAGE 75

PAGE 73:
A) RECENTLY GIVEN BIRTH POSTAL

(from page 77 & 100)

Bahahahahahahahahahahaha! Wrong. Answer. Mate. What sort of a moron would actively give unwelcome advice of any nature to a bunch of severely sleep deprived, recently birth-giving Mothers? The inner monologue of the entire room can no longer be contained and you are the first to comment.

"Actually, no thank you. I just want some sleep."

Then another...

"Are you lactating? How's about a little shush."

And another...

"We're the ones with the boobs! If we aren't asking session is over."

Then free for all...

"Saboteur!"

"I just want you to stop talking. Please. Just stop."

Superdick's head seems to bobble like a buoy in rough waters as the barrage of comments bulldoze over him. It sounds like a vent session at a feminist rally and you feel a tiny bit for him. It's short lived.

"Sorry you feel that way. My wife and I have done *our* research and found..." and he actually lists his *"best practice"* findings along with a plethora of acts *Wifey* will supposedly do. It all sounds suspiciously like demands, rather than choices. *Superdick* seems like a super control freak whose only way to maintain a shred of that control (in what is probably the first situation he has had none) is to dictate how things are going to roll with *his* baby.

You adjust your position on the inflatable arse cushion Green Man loaned you – an initiation gift to the Bum Nut Club. The shift of your swollen gelada butt causes a surge of pain, but even that can't distract you from the enigma that is *Superdick*. He would totally be the first to die in a horror film. The annoying arsehole killed off at the start of a movie. The character an audience cheer for collective joy when they are exterminated by aliens, or disintegrated by an arsehole-eating virus, or mauled by a peckish pack of she-wolves on a *tosspot* only diet. Unfortunately, there are no alien infected wolf packs with special dietary requirements present at the BREAST FEEDING, SUPPORT & SELF-CARE FOR THE NEW MOTHER session today. Shame. *Superdick's* gob-smacking prattle is super relentless.

The poor munted Mum looks mortified and digs her talons into his skin. The rest of the group start hobbling toward him like a herd of hungry zombies who feed off the blood of overly opinionated know-all's. The Midwife diffuses the slightly psychotic situation.

"Yes okay, sir. That is quite enough from you. I think we're done here and just in time for morning tea. Well done, ladies. Go and rest. You've certainly earned it."

You all slowly disperse back to the rooms. You think about that couple for a long time and try to see it from every angle. *Superdick's* intentions are probably from a positive space and he should be commended for giving a shit to take the time to educate himself with so-called *breast practices*. However, his enthusiasm may come at the cost of his Wife's mental wellbeing and possibly their child's and maybe even the family unit. Truly, you are all for balance and equality, but, unless he hangs with seahorses, maybe he could be more sensitive to the audiences he chooses to roll his podium out to. The unique experience of giving birth – with our amazing and unbelievably complex bodies – can only be understood by those who have gone through it, something *Superdick* could never fully comprehend.

You hop down from your box and bring Bumbalina in for a nuzzle. In one huge snort bub reminds you **she** is the only thing that is important and your exhaustion disappears along with thoughts of *Superdick's* possible mammary envy. You burp your lumpy little lady and change her tiny bot, then you both fall into a blissful sleep that lasts exactly twenty eight minutes and ten seconds. The photographer has returned to take photos of Missy. Her last disaster-filled session consisted of sporadic crying, weird faces and a nappy full of nasty. Thankfully, bub sleeps deeply and many angelic shots are snapped.

You settle back in for nap attempt number two thousand and eleven when the phone rings. It's Green Man letting you know he's on his way. Fan-fCking-tastic. Information he could have shared with his actual presence when he arrived in the flesh. You let him know you don't need a blow by blow account of his whereabouts. Cold. As. Ice. Sleepless you is quite the charmer and unfortunately poor Green Man cops the wrath intended for *Superdick*. This really sets the tone for the evening, which is supposed to be a romantic one. Candle lit dinner should be interesting.

GO TO: PAGE 29

PAGE 74:
B) HEAD HOME

(from page 38)

The second you are in the car you lose it. Hysterically. Thankfully, by the time you arrive home you have gotten at least a quarter of it out of your system. Green Man phoned ahead to warn the family of the unfortunate change of circumstances. They meet and greet you with all their beautiful, warm positivity and are glad you are "okay" now you are home where they can fuss over you. Which they do and it's lovely to be with your comforting kin.

But all you want to do is empty your boobs, have a shower, wash your filthy hair, scrub that wretched hospital off your skin and cry yourself to sleep. Which you do. The sleep is black and dreamless. It's so deep that when you awake the bed is saturated with milk that desperately needed the hungry mouth of your babe to drink.

GO TO: PAGE 72

PAGE 75:
A) BACK TO BUB

(from page 61 & 72)

The next day you return. You've expressed a whole lot of beautiful milk and by your careful calculations the boobasbord should be ready for bubs thirsty lips on arrival. The full night of sleep helped a bit too and you are feeling slightly more hopeful at the prospect of bringing bundles home. Green Man gently warns against getting those hopes up, but you are optimistic the test results will be back based on your very limited knowledge of hospital pathology. You are a firm believer in the power of positivity and even in this uncertain state, haven't completely lost faith in miracles – it is Christmas after all.

You try and rush (as fast as your body will allow) to your babe who is sleeping soundly. No one is near him. In fact, your Mister Moo is on the outskirts like he has leprosy. You let it go and cuddle him, taking in a glow of love like never before. You know they don't smile at this stage, but his little mouth curls up and you snuggle close.

S2 is on duty and barely acknowledges you. That would normally have you doing backflips like a trained poodle for her approval, but right now you don't care. You turn your back and slowly pace over to the window. You cheek to cheek Mini Man and Mum-jig, blissfully content. The sorrow of yesterday is replaced by those magical maternal waves that wash over your entire being and you decide then and there you will never be forced to leave your child again.

You sit down to feed him. The expressing gave you some confidence and you are determined to get this whole latching thing going ASAP. But, when you put breast to babe he turns away and is not remotely hungry.

"Oh, Mrs Man, he probably won't need a feed. We had to give him formula. He went through all your milk and just would not settle," *S1* calls out and your nostrils immediately flare. Your *Super Smell* can sniff out bullshit from great distances and her breath reeks of it. You thought you left plenty of milk. Did they shove a bottle in his gob for every little squawk? Or perhaps they didn't want to comfort him for other reasons? Green Man told them to ring at any time and he would bring you in. You quietly seethe. The formula no doubt soothed and nourished your son when suffering babies held priority over him – a healthy baby most likely crying out for his mother. Because there was nothing wrong with him. Because he shouldn't have been there. Because this entire mess could have been dissolved if just *one* person would have listened to you.

S2 summons *S1* and you can't help but sense it's to get her away from you. She leaves you be, but not alone. You kiss bubby-boo again, breathe in his scent and wonder how much of your frazzled angst he is taking in. If there is such a thing as an aura – yours would look like a jolting mass of electrically charged squiggles. You feel powerless to stop the toxic gunk surging into bub and reluctantly hand him over to Green Man. You take a walk.

Thankfully, none of the babies are in the critical zone, though nearly all are without their Mums for much of the time. This only intensifies your guilt for being in the ward with your low risk/non-life threatened *patient*. You gently pat a few tiny backs and sing some soothing lullabies as you pass, then look around like you're in a Margaret Atwood novel. It probably is discouraged and may drive the poor things crazy – you being both the only real food source and comfort in the room – but the staff are unable to tend to all of them all of the time and it doesn't seem right to let them *cry it out*. You just hope they can't sense your turmoil. They don't and instantly calm. You have always had a gift for baby whispering and for these few moments it is an honour to soothe these little darlings' suffering with your Mummyness.

Of the few parents you do come across – some distressed, some calm – most are there for premmies. As you cuddle your whale-child you feel like a fraud. A couple of the Mums can't touch their infants, let alone hold them. You sense their heartbreak and are hyper-aware you are not experiencing a similar trauma. The shame intensifies even more whenever you nurse, or interact with your bountiful bub without a panel of glass between you. The guilt is overwhelming. Paranoia sets in and you wonder if they know. The few conversations you manage to engage in lead to questions and you sense their suspicions.

"Why is your baby here?"

"Is he prem?"

Clearly his size is quite the glaring giveaway that he did not arrive early and you cringe as the confusion flashes across their faces.

*Well, what **is** wrong with him then?* It's like you can read their thoughts. You feel sick answering. The reactions are all the same. Polite then concerned. Their natural instinct is to protect their own infants who are suffering, or high risk, or both, or worse. These women are in the same headspace as you, but they have every reason to be. Your child is not remotely in any danger, or at risk of death, nor *is* he a risk, or a threat to anyone else. Contrary to the imaginary symptoms that have him impounded – your reaction to all of it is **very real**. This cluster-fCk ferris-wheel just amps up the self-loathing as you plunge deeper into Victimsville. They can't hide their body language which turns from you and your baby even with cordial subtlety. You are physically and telepathically segregated. You pull bub closer to shield him as they shield themselves from the two of you. The staff seem to know it's going on, yet offer no comfort. Whether they have pegged you or not you feel like your baby has been doomed by a mother who is nothing but a *Sinister* carrying slut. Ostracised, vilified and dirty.

There is little time to process any of that. You are still a walking milk dispenser and your boobs overflow with the feed bub missed – the one where he should have been nursing in the comfort of your judgement-free home.

On top of that, your baby whispering efforts have dissipated and the mere presence of you sets off a frenzy through the unit. You are like a seeping poppy in an opium den no one can tap into.

You try feeding bub again, but trying to master your wayward, sabotaging mammaries is disastrous. You have eff-all idea what you're doing and are neither prepared, nor properly equipped. The expressing confidence quickly evaporates. There's been no time alone with your infant for trial and error of any sort, and you are shockingly clueless on what to pack when leaving the house for all the parenting *just-in-cases* that only an efficiently packed nappy-bag would sufficiently service. You are usually such a flexible, go-with-the-flow, adaptable beast, but this is some deep-end stuff you did not expect so soon, or so solo. All the reading and education in the world does not prepare you for real events and no one here has the time, or the will to offer an encouraging smile, let alone advice on what is – in comparison to the unit – very, very trivial. That doesn't stop you feeling like everyone is watching and holding up score cards.

You wonder if you'll ever get the hang of breastfeeding and quietly sink deeper into your doubting hovel. You try to navigate bub in one arm with pins and needles in the other. You soon discover the pretty breast pads you cluelessly purchased months ago, leak almost instantly. Because of the lack of bag prep, you have to borrow a tiny muslin cloth which you repeatedly drop, awkwardly revealing yourself and immediately feel smothered by a surge of dismay and embarrassment. Mini-Man seems just as frustrated with your antics and protests loudly, turning a few heads. You panic more. In the one space you should thrive you feel useless, intimidated and monstrously unco. Still, no one offers a shred of comfort, or a kind word. It doesn't take long for you to be a mess again and as much as you want to stay, Green Man insists on taking you away from this mentally taxing space.

Time for lunch.

WHICH ONE?
A) HOSPITAL CAFETERIA: PAGE 88
B) GO OUT: PAGE 15

PAGE 76:
ALL ABOARD/DOWN WITH THE SHIP

(from page 8)

You have never experienced such hideous sickness in your entire life. You want to die. In fact, at one point you reckon you are dying. Even when sitting perfectly still and upright it feels like the room is one big bastard boat rocking back and forth, up and down, side to bloody side on perpetually rough seas.

To accompany the morning sickness fun you have also developed a superhuman sense of smell and your **Wonder Nostrils** are apparently on overdrive. Unfortunately, no matter where you are it seems every person on the planet is cooking meat and you despise yourself for every burger, steak and sausage your shmackers have ever wrapped themselves around. Vile! The urge to hug a cow is strong and you make a note (forgetting it seventy five seconds later) to never again take the piss out of fakon bacon. Not that *that* smells much better right now. Pork = Bad. Fake Pork = Bad + What-The-FCkery?

People take pity on you and every second woman who has ever been pregnant peddles their barley sugars to cure your incurable ailment. You try, but it's like sucking on saccharin flavoured glass. Your Dad even steps in and gives you some of his ginger chews that nearly burn your face off mid-munch. Thankfully, Bestie (who is conveniently pregnant at the same time) offers you some ginger beer.

The remedy works and is your main anti-hurl-go-to for the next few months.

The band-aidy beer is only capable of so much. Hiding the vomit inducing oven bun whilst navigating your newfound captaincy on the good ship *spews-a-lot* without raising Green Man's suspicions, is quite the quandary. The first couple of weeks you got away with general under-the-weather illnesses, but you've now reached piss-pulling, sickie heights. If Green Man is well versed on the bubonic plague you may have to come clean about the faux disease-causing alien spawn floating around inside you. The moment of truth is nigh. But how to break the baby news?

BEER. THE NON-GINGER KIND.

At least he can navigate himself through the whole thing in a numbed state. Regardless, you can't go on like this. He needs to know.

DO YOU:
A) BEERPALOOZA: PAGE 71
B) SOBRIETY: PAGE 57

PAGE 77:
SUPERDICK HAS SOME ANNOYING SUPER POWERS

(from page 113)

As hard as you try to ignore *Superdick*, he is one of those people who are oblivious to what's going on until it karate chops them in the face. In the storm brewing climate of the BREASTFEEDING, SUPPORT & SELF-CARE FOR THE NEW MOTHER session – there is a high probability of someone delivering an uppercut to his chin very soon.

To add to the collective irritation, *SD* has another really annoying superpower. He is a constant question-asking-commenter – code for: *Everyone-must-marvel-at-how-much-I-know*. Oh my-my-my-good-lolly-golly-gosh do you effing loathe unnecessary question askers, random commenters and general self-indulgent timewasters even when you *do* have an iota of sanity in storage. It takes every ounce of what little effort you have left not to roll your eyeballs out of their sockets every time he opens his super dickery mouth. There are soooo many ridiculous comments you nearly tear the foam from the armchair. Thankfully, it's not just you. At first the Midwife is impressed by his thirst for knowledge until he starts questioning her. Much sideward glancing. Much flabbergastment.

His poor partner has nearly melted into a coma, but is brought back to life by the sounds of knuckle-crunching echoing off the walls.

Everyone seems to snarl as she reads the situation in seconds and gently puts her hand on his arm.

"Enough now," she whispers, but *SD* ignores her. He seems irritated at the suggestion and continues peppering. The Midwife looks ready to roll up her sleeves and even the calm, supportive Fathers grunt at his arrogance. Your inner monologue is officially off the chain and you are a little concerned that once it escapes out loud, security may get involved. You just want this session to end so you can pass out in the blazing light of your room. Even the late-night disco ward would be better than this.

But *SD* continues.

The Midwife gives him every polite hint to shut the hell up and still he waffles on like a narcissistic dipstick. His partner reaches out again, but this time she's well over it.

"Just let them finish. I don't think anyone wants to hear it, love," she says and if a round of applause was wince-free you would have given her a standing ovation.

For the first time since he arrives *SD* looks up and acknowledges there are actual humans in the room other than himself.

"Well, this benefits all of you too. You should *want* to hear it."

Oh dear. It's postals all round.

PICK A POSTAL:
A) RECENTLY GIVEN BIRTH POSTAL: PAGE 73
B) ZOMBIE APOCALYPSE POSTAL: PAGE 100

PAGE 78:
B) SIT BACK AND RELAX

(from page 10)

Haha! Yeah. Nah. You've witnessed many a woman with an uncanny ability to float through life with a calm, rational and zenny aura. Where everything they touch falls naturally and perfectly into place with minimal effort or stress. *You,* however have always been on the polar end of that foreign spectrum. Your aura resembles more of an electric shock of neurotic hysteria when charged with the insane tasks you attempt to undertake. You tend to juggle too many balls way beyond your skill set with a *chuck-into-basket-throw-basket-drop-the-lot-repeat* approach. A very headless chook kind of ethos. But not this time! Not with this huge milestone. You will not pass this disorderly and dysfunctional turd onto your infant. You poke your tummy like it's a doorbell.

"Not on my watch, little one," you whisper reassuringly. That loopy affirmation won't last longer than a day, but you are determined to have a crack. How hard can this organised, responsible, reliable, sensible and stable adult stuff be? You soon find out as your former track-keeping husband and only means of accountability – is now a fully functional boozer and temporarily out of the game. *Typical.* You huff. You huff a lot lately (non-fume high). It's your new vibey thing and if you're going to vibe at all it might as well be a practical one. There shall be much huffing that will last long after bub is born. For now you're on your own, Huffy. Huff it up.

Grab some scented pens and open your reluctant arms to the world of list taking.

GO TO: PAGE 21

PAGE 79:
B) TAILS: MIRACLE ON CAESAREAN STREET

(from page 12 & 107)

Green Man is being prepped for surgery. Unfortunately, the rest of your entourage are not allowed in. You cry again. Mum smothers you with so many smooches it almost distracts you from the sour turn of events. Normally the power of *Mum kisses* solves everything. She wipes your tears. She squeezes you tight. Your hero. Your source of strength and go-to for so many of life's booboos, always with an empathetic ear and a gentle nudge when you've lost your way. You wish you could be her happy little shadow again, safe at her side this one last time.

"You can do it, darling. I believe in you," she whispers through her own tears and you both sob. This is one booboo she can't help fix.

Your Aunty follows suit with kisses and sweet comforting words and you are so grateful to have them both at the birth of your son. You wish your Nan was here to make it the magical trio. Your idols. Your first initiation to girl power, to humour, to grace. You wave at them like you are five years old again, when they were your very own celebrities and you their biggest fan. As they leave the tear flood arrives.

"It's goodbye from us too now, lovey," says Brighid. She gently rubs your arm as Juliette flanks you on the other side.

"What? No! Can't you come with me?"

"Sadly, we can't go with you this time, lassie."

"You'll be fine in there. You are strong. We are so proud of you."

"Oh no, Juliette! Will you still pass even though you didn't deliver my baby?" you ask and they both laugh and hug you again.

"Of course she will, lovey! With honours after this lot!"

"I've got you to thank. Now don't worry about all that. You just…"

"Sorry ladies. Time to go," calls an orderly who turns you ready to roll. Brighid and Juliette wave like they're farewelling close family. They wave with the love of a Mother who has a million things to do, but keeps waving knowing her kids will watch her until she is nothing but a speck. They wave as you are pushed through another set of doors that swing back and forth, back and forth. They wave until the doors finally stand still and you no longer see one another. After hours and hours of being in their kind, supportive presence – there is no more waving. There is no more them. There is nothing but a bright corridor and a pleasant stranger. And just like that Brighid and Juliette's brief, but mammoth part in your story ends, forever. It feels like you will never see, never speak and never be in the company of that beautiful pair ever again. The thought is devastatingly empty.

"Someone will be here soon. Don't worry, you'll be okay," the orderly reassures, parking the bed against the cold wall. You give him a – *No worries. I'll be fine. Just half a baby head hanging from my flim flam, but all good here…* nod. The second he goes you quietly ugly-cry in the very silent corridor. Alone. Thoughts of C-section scenarios fill your head. You had prepared for pain, but not for being cut open. You are scared. All the *what-ifs* casually waltz on in as an intergalactic mind war ensues. The goodies put up their negative thought shields against a barrage of scars, blood and death lasers. The good guys triumph and you are rewarded with a full breath of antiseptic laden air. Nothing can defeat images of a baby safe in your arms, no matter how he arrives into them, or what your aftermath will be. You look around and squint.

Shit it's bright. Why do corridors have to be so bloody bright? It's not like they're operating in here... or are they?

You let that panic slide. Even a fluorescent passageway is better than giving birth curbside with the towel festival of last night. Your train of crazy thoughts are interrupted by a new anaesthetist who has served everyone's spine in the hospital, except yours. He's wearing a flamboyant bandana. It's brighter than the hallway and the only colour you've seen in hours. He whistles while he wheels you into a room stocked with lots of medical crap, and you lay bemused that his cliché actually exists.

"You're not crying are you?" he questions and grins charmingly. You cannot fathom why someone would bother to charm anyone in your soggy, sop-ridden state.

"No. Maybe. A little bit," you respond, unsure if he's taking the piss to make you feel better, or is really irritated by sooking.

"Come on now. Your part is easy! All you have to do is lay there and look at my mug. Now keep still while we top you up," he says with a thick ocker accent. "Doc is just finishing up and we'll have you in and out soon," he continues his one-sided banter as the lower half of your body feels like it has disappeared. It's not numbness, it's nothingness. A weird mish-mash of relief, fear, disappointment and impatience swirl around the bits that still work and as much as his distractions are appreciated, you wish *Bandana Man* would shut up and let you rest a moment. He must sense your exhaustion and hums quietly. You briefly close your eyes and awaken to a kiss on the hand. Green Man has finally returned dressed in scrubs and you've never been happier to see him. There is actual colour in his cheeks other than *shades of swamp*. Looks like the toast and milo was a good thing. The anaesthetist also lights up at the sight of him and the calm, quiet mood is soon gone as his laughter ricochets off the glass cabinets in the dog-box transit-room.

"Ah, yes! The man of the moment! You're the talk of the ward, mate. You have absolutely made my day with your efforts."

"Yep. Cheers," Green Man reluctantly responds.

"And they were right! You actually match the scrubs! Gold!"

"Yeah thanks, mate. This is really helping," he answers with a semi-smirk as *Bandana Man* laughs louder, genuinely elated to be in the presence of what appears to be Green Man's newfound celebrity. He even calls a passerby to join in on the piss-taking. More and more staff come to point, laugh, take selfies and give Green Man the big thumbs up. He shuns them all and leans into you.

"Are you okay? How's the pain?" he asks like he is seeing you for the first time.

"Gone. You?"

"Still drunk I think, but much better after the food."

"Awesome. Welcome back," you tease and giggle at his town drunk crown.

"I just want to meet our boy."

"Me too," you reply. He kisses your cheek.

"And you will, missy. It's time," *Bandana Man* announces, flashing his pearlies and you're off again. He rolls you into a much bigger, sparser room filled with bustle, lights and metal. There is a heavy veil of no-nonsense in the air that will soon be filled with an intoxicating scent you will never, ever forget. Blood. Like an iron factory. At least it's not shit.

The surgeon probes then steps back and speaks to the staff who immediately scurry about like ants. Green Man is pulled aside, but you can't hear what's being said, so you hold your breath and presume the worse. He soon returns to your side.

"What's wrong? Is the baby all right?"

"The baby's fine. He's turned. The Doc is going to pull him out naturally, but they need to do it now. There's something... pelvis... something... cord... something... blur... something... clang... something else..." The clattering, the bustling, the sheer exhaustion have Green Man sounding like an old TV set that needs a good whack to tune him into your frazzled frequency. The frivolity of the birthing suite has long gone, but you sense something else. Panic. Not hysteria, but a definite sense of urgency. Green Man can feel it too. You look up at his face that is inches from yours and notice the change in his demeanour. Nothing sobers a man up quicker than an unscheduled wife and child **_Plan B_**.

"Is everything okay? Is the baby okay?"

"It's all right. He knows what he's doing... he's like a damned ninja... fCk he's good!" Green Man fans out over the surgeon as you stare at him blankly.

"Ninja? What's going on?"

"It's good. It's good. There's just... so much blood..."

"What?!?"

"It's normal. It's normal," he strokes your head way too hard and sugar coats nothing. You admire his enthusiasm. He's calling the birth like a Jiu-jitsu match and you half expect a tiny street fighter to pop out at any moment ready for a brawl. You forget it immediately, just desperate to hear the one sound you've been waiting so long for. _Surgeon Ninja_ says something instead.

"Okay. Push now."

Ay? What was that? Did he speak? It's like a moth's breath. You look up confused until his words are echoed like a Conga line through each assisting nurse, student and every miscellaneous random in the room.

"It's time to push, Mrs Man!"

"Oh… okay… I… can't… feel… anything. It's… not… working…"

"Yes it is, Mrs Man and you're doing great. Have a rest for a moment."

"Okay. Push," *Moth-Man-Ninja-Hands* barely whispers again.

"Mrs Man, another big push for us now… very good. Great job…"

You do what you think must be pushing because it seems to be getting a positive reaction from the crowd, but the truth is you can't feel jack shit down there. You soon push so well that not only does a child drop out, but your haemorrhoids get their jazz hands on permanently outside your bum. Just like your vagina, neither will ever be the same again. Green Man would nickname them *dangleberries,* while you will refer to them as an inconvenient and literal pain in the arse. But, at this stage you are none the wiser and your only concern is seeing your baby and hearing him cry.

Suddenly, Green Man's face flushes a deep red and tears stream down his cheeks.

"He's out… yep… yep… yeah… he's out!" he calls, shifting to cricket commentary. He smiles and kisses you repeatedly. Some relief arrives. You smile back and try to see beyond the curtain and clanging and blood to catch a glimpse of your baby boy, but he is whisked away. The panic returns. The staff block your view of what you presume is your baby. You catch sight of something small and blue. There is no noise. You can't take your eyes from it. So you hold your breath again for what seems an age. Toxic thoughts of the worst outcome penetrate through you like poison and time seems to freeze. Then it's there. A big, bold, beautiful cry launches from the tiny mouth of your babe and it fills the starkness like colourful musical notes from an old cartoon. Everyone collectively breathes. Green Man is summonsed and his face illuminates. He strokes the little arm of his son and beams like a planet.

"He looks like me," he gushes loudly and the room chuckles. You lie back like a hacked moose and relish in his joy. After nine months of trying to convince Green Man that all the bullshit he held dear would disappear once he saw his son – it finally happened and in a far more divine and emblematic way than you could ever have imagined. Sure, you had to drive yourself in and nearly die, but it was all worth it just for the reaction you knew he had in him all along. Green Man can't take his eyes from his Mini-Man, so you leave him to it – happy he is in love. You rest your head back on the pillow and stare at the ceiling that may or may not be moving.

"Hey now, Mrs Man. Someone wants to meet you too," says one of the many lovely staff. You open your eyes to see your boy set across your chest. For the briefest moment he looks up and you lock eyes on each other. Everything disappears. All that exists in the universe right now is you, your child and the warm coating of love that wraps you both in its protective cloak. Nothing else matters. You finally have a baby – your baby. He frowns as if to say *"Mornin Mum. FYI – maybe your pelvis wouldn't have been such an issue if you'd laid off the bullets!"* He farts and falls asleep. You stare and you stare and stare some more, and the little girl who knew she was always going to have kids sings out for joy to the stratosphere that she just gave birth to a grumpy, feisty, street fighting, eighty year old little man. You kiss him, and stroke his wrinkly face as he scrunches his nose with every touch. You joke that he probably just wants his pipe and slippers and to be left the hell alone.

As they pack you up and prepare for the next birther, everyone smiles and offer kind well-dones. Even *Bandana Man* pats your head like proud *Farmer Flamboyant* praising his prize cow for birthing the next county fair champion. He gives you a wink.

"Oh, okay. I'll allow tears of joy just this once," he whispers. You smile up at him and again find yourself overwhelmed with gratitude to be in the hands of such beautiful professionals. You let the tears flow. The surgeon comes over and pats your arm too. He smiles at the baby and then at you.

"Very well done," he says at a volume only whales could hear. He mentions the baby scraped his forehead on your pelvis as he was pulling him out. He apologises saying it was unavoidable, though nothing to worry about and **the wound would heal quickly**. You're just glad it's all done and thank the exceptional humans over and over and over again. You were one of a long list of women being whipped in and out like cattle and you will never forget what transpired between everyone in the room when *Plan B* nearly became end game.

You are whisked out without the chance to farewell anyone. Not the softly spoken surgeon, not *Bandana Man*, nor the many kind and encouraging staff and students, who in the coming years dissipate into faceless memories. You wish you could have thanked them all individually. Such a bizarre experience to hand over your life and your baby's to strangers and never even learn their names. The normalisation of such a monumental thing seems surreal.

You leave the space that housed you for the last twenty hours or so for the final time and arrive in a room, alone. Having been repeatedly told private rooms were like hen's teeth, you manage an exhausted, *yay*. Enjoy that microscopically thin little fishy scale of good luck. That will be the last of it for a long while.

IT'S OVER! TIME TO REST
AND ENJOY THIS NEW BEING.

GO TO: PAGE 2

PAGE 80:
THE UNFINISHED BABY ROOM

(from page 111)

Seriously? How hard is it? Twenty one point twelve minutes after you found out the sex you were ready to get cracking on the baby room. Green Man's one-time offer to paint the nursery evaporated when he realised you would not be talked out of assisting. Not that he wasn't keen on a partnered project, but your work ethic notoriously never did mirror his borderline psychotic level of craftsmanship. His is a skill set and ethos that can only be equalled by alien life forms with obsessive compulsive perfectionism. Yours is more of a sporadic, eager, yet, hyperactive octopus and Green Man has bugger-all faith in your methods, delivery or ability. You can't blame him. Most tasks involving you and tools have a bit of the dodge to them. Fuffing about with trivial things like uneven edges, or random left over screws is just a distraction from finishing. For you it's a win if shit stays standing longer than an hour and a trip to emergency is avoided.

As you drag out the paint equipment with DIY enthusiasm – a sudden shadow casts its naysaying gloom.

HIM: What are you doing?

YOU: Time to paint the room.

HIM: Yeah I'll do it… soon.

YOU: No you won't. You'll wait until the night before I'm due.

HIM: I promise I won't. Now hand it over.

FAIRY TALE TIME

Once upon a time there were two dung beetles. The first would rise early and locate the best dung. His patience and craftsmanship were supreme as he pushed and rolled steaming turds with precision and flair. However, he would often procrastinate on chores requiring that high level of perfectionism. These unrealistic expectations would drain his energy reserves resulting in half-completed jobs that cluttered the home and created a grumpy dung demeanor. Being a perfectionist took its toll on Dung Beetle 1 and eventually on DB 2 and their little family of shit rollers.

Dung Beetle 2 had no time for craft-honing and focused on getting the job done. She did not seek a level of unattainable perfection because she knew it would take away from living. As a result her life was often chaotic and unorganised. She too was a superior poo pusher, but not remotely picky. DB 2 was content with her lot even though her methods were corner cutty and things would often break down. She valued her mental stability and just got on with the rolling of shit, the getting of shit, and the giving of few shits.

Ironically, the two fell in love and had a complicated, but fruitful marriage. Unfortunately, whilst procrastinating over the quality of a poo pad – Dung Beetle 1 was eaten by a cunning ibis. Dung Beetle 2 donned mourning black for the remainder of her life, which ended a decade later when the home she had built collapsed and crushed her to dung death.

Moral? Poor craftsmanship and a fCk-free work ethic will add at least ten years to your life, but probably be the cause of ending it.

THE END

Back to the nursery…

YOU: I can help.

HIM: You can mask the room.

YOU: Give me a brush and I'll help you paint.

HIM: ………… The taping is really important.

YOU: Who do you think you're fooling?

HIM: ……………

YOU: Babe?

HIM: ……….. *hands you tape*

YOU: So I'm tape wench?

HIM: I think it's better for everyone.

YOU: How dare you. Lemme help.

HIM: You rush too much.

YOU: I'll admit I may be a mite slap-dash sometimes, but I get the job done without dicking around.

HIM: "Slap dash?" You're like a hyperactive cricket. You jump in with no planning or prep and I always have to re-do what you've done!

YOU: I am deeply offended. This is discrimination. Me and the crickets shall fight it!

HIM: You do that. You gonna tape?

YOU: Shove that tape…

You curse. A lot. In the final months you curse some more for not painting the room whilst Green Man was gallivanting up a booze storm and your grasshopper game was still stellar. Alas, that ship was torpedoed thanks to the recent stool balancing escapades. You are not only ordered to cut the physical crap out, but are hijacked by a body that is giving you little choice than to rest like medicinal fungi. Building cots, drawers, change tables, painting walls, putting up curtains, organising closets, clothes and finding homes for all the baby crap is officially out of your hands and not remotely being entertained by the rarely present Green Man.

Just like the baby shower, you have been prepping, planning and hoarding the baby room stuff since the beginning of the pregnancy. Hours upon hours upon hours of images have been saved and catalogued and you are now more than ready to bring all 28,1276 of those Pinterest visions to life. Problem is the nursery you have built your baby room dreams around – one nestled into a billion dollar mountainside ranch style bungalow – doesn't really match the three by four dog box in the dodgy suburb where you and Green Man reside. Rather than fresh forest scents, northern lights and gorgeous snowcapped ranges – you have robot towers, snowcapped meth labs and the pretty lights of frequent police raids.

For now the three bits of tape and four paint sample strokes is going to have do for the nursery. Just as predicted Green Man and his cape of procrastination flew far, far away from the chore he was never that keen in doing. Painting walls eggshell neutral and assembling million dollar cots is a reality he continues to ignore from the safe view of his rectum. A view he will soon have no choice but to crawl out from and embrace his leading role.

Let the circus begin!

TIME FOR THE THIRD TRIMESTER!

GO TO: PART 3 – PAGE 50

PAGE 81:
A) CALL BESTIE

(from page 14)

Well done. Probably the best decision you could have made. By the time you finish up the preparation madness you are a haggard mess. It's late and if you call at this hour Bestie will know something is up, so you text her to take up her rent-a-fam offer. Lucky you did. In the morning you awake to discover you can barely move. She waddles in with her family of angels who take over in a most well-oiled way.

They look at the extravaganza you've already achieved. The young ones are amazed and shower you with praise, but the wiser women raise a collective eyebrow and move suspiciously onto the few chores left. Bestie is not fooled either and orders you to sit on the only chair you can comfortably fit into. For once you do as you're told.

The baby shower is a success. Besides going to the toilet you pretty much stay put, and are generously showered with gifts, love and joy.

Once everyone has left you get up to farewell Bestie and her merrymaking band of magicians – when a sudden pain spears through you. Bestie is having none of it and orders an escort in the Angel-mobile where they drive you to the hospital toot-sweet.

GO TO: PAGE 42

PAGE 82:
THE DRUNKEN HUSBAND

(from page 22)

Green Man is being lured to the sunken bar that is your Uncle's booze cave. Many a man has succumbed to the tantalising delights stored within. Big, bold, brass men who fall prey to the alluring saloon doors only to find themselves passed out drooling underneath the pool table at eight in the morning wondering how the hell they got there.

Big, bold, brass are not words one would attach to Green Man. Logical, sensible and one-not-known-for-his-massive-consumption-of-alcohol are definitely more suited. Non-skuller-of-copious-amounts-of-red-wine would also be a fitting description and one that should have been adhered to this night. But, with you and your impending guts of life-changing doom parading around – his less than eager demeanour is noticed by most of your relatives. Never ones to shy away from getting legless and piss-taking for hours – they hone in on Green Man with crates of vintage

Château La FCked-Faced

You've seen it all before. They love this type of chicanery and smile gleefully at the nervous Father-to-be. Green Man tries to hide it, but they grind him down until he openly admits to crapping his dacks about things to come. So, he gets absolutely maggoted – because he's done nothing but that for nine months and why stop now when the apocalyptic moment is nigh?

You ponder entering the lion's den and suggest he slow down. You are overdue and could blow at any second. Then again, he'll be balls deep in breast milk and baby poo soon enough. Might as well let him enjoy these final child-free moments. As if you'll go into labour tonight.

Right?

DO YOU:
A) SLOW DOWN: PAGE 16
B) LET HIM GO: PAGE 41

PAGE 83:
B) AQUA AEROBICS

(from page 18)

Oh lordy. It's like watching a plucked chicken broiling in the slow cooker. You insist on wearing *normal* bathers which are nothing too risqué. At least your ten tonne titties are safely strapped in and hopefully your atomic wedgie will loosen as the lycra is eaten away by the insane level of chlorine. You have joined aqua-aerobics, which makes zero sense as you loathe aerobics in any form when you're not carrying a child. But, you have purposefully made yourself join a group class knowing you'll last one second if left to do laps on your own. You manage the first ten minutes and are oblivious to what's happening after that as you go into rotisserie mode – bobbing round and round lapping up the weightless freedom.

Basty basty she goes.

All is light and floaty and ouch free for a blissful moment until the aerobics instructor – an unapologetically cantankerous woman – stops the entire class and orders them to set you adrift. Rude. You breast stroke towards an exit when you remember this is not the swimming pool you used to frequent. There is no lovely faux shore to gracefully trawl yourself back on to dry land. This pool is like an outdoor community watering hole installed in the thirties and your only exit is a rusty old ladder so deep it requires much stamina to reach the first rung.

Later that night you hurl your disintegrating bathers at Green Man's gigglemug as he insists on pressing your soggy buttons.

"How many people did it take to get you out?"

"Nine. Plus the big crane thingy they use for the giant inflatables," you mumble. He buckles over. You ignore him and chafe away to your kitchen comfort zone where seven bottles of *Lik-Wid-Choc* are perfectly lined in a row. They reach their delicious arms out to comfort you, patting your shoulder and stroking your chlorinated hair.

"*There, there. Safe now. Drink up,*" they probably don't whisper.

"Yes, my chocolatey friends. Yes I will," you insanely respond and chug back five bottles without breathing, then settle into the couch where you remain for the next few days in a sugar coma. Just as you ease into never moving again – celebration season is upon you and it is no surprise that nothing in your wardrobe remotely fits. You hug an empty bottle and may or may not shove your fingers inside it like a bear scabbing honey from a beehive.

"*Worry tomorrow. You missed a bit,*" the near empty bottle may or may not whisper.

"Yes," is all you say and shove in one of those bamboo eco-straws and suck the remaining chocolate out with glee.

GO TO: PAGE 31

PAGE 84:
A) TELL HIM STRAIGHT AWAY

(from page 1)

YOU: Hi babe. I've got some exciting news.

HIM: Okay.

YOU: Can you guess?

HIM: Nup.

YOU: Wanna try?

HIM: ……… *crickets*……. *white noise*…… *tumbleweeds*……

YOU: I'm PREGNANT!

HIM: ………………………………………………………………

YOU: Hello? Hello? Babe?

HIM: …… You're fCking with me?

YOU: Um, no. But I think I may be glowing.

HIM: What?

YOU: You know *the glow?*

HIM: How did this happen?

YOU: *The glow*?

HIM: No! Th…. is?

YOU: We had sex.

HIM: Not enough! I don't understand?

YOU: We actively stopped using contraception.

HIM: But, so soon?

YOU: Where are you going with this?

HIM: (*high toney*) We were supposed to have heaps more sex! That's the good part about the whole baby making thing right?

YOU: We can still have sex.

HIM: Yeah right.

YOU: How did you manage to make this amazing milestone about your penis?

HIM: …………………..

YOU: Hello?

HIM: ………… You're right. I'm sorry… But are you really sure?

YOU: Are you shitting me right now?

HIM: I mean... Don't you need to do some blood tests?

YOU: I will, but a 'yes' indication on the piss-piece usually means no returns.

HIM: Brilliant.

YOU: Hello?

HIM: …………………………..

YOU: Hello? *You bang the phone like they do in the movies – like it is actually attached to a cord and an operator is on the other end.* It would probably be best if you make your way over to the happy-happy baby party I've got going on.

HIM: Yeah… sorry babe. I just can't believe it happened… so… quick.

YOU: Have you met my family? All seven thousand of them? I was born to breed!

HIM: Apparently so.

YOU: At least you know you're not packing sleepers down there! A silver lining if ever there was one!

HIM: True.

YOU: And the whole *we're going to have a baby thing* is kind of cool too… right?

HIM: Yeah. Na. Of course. Yep. It is. Really cool babe. Amazing news…

He trails off to the Never-Never.

DO YOU:
A) WRAP IT UP: PAGE 10
B) KEEP WAFFLING: PAGE 64

PAGE 85:
SAVE VS SPEND

(from page 109)

You barely make it home from the eXpo in one piece and are loaded up with bags on bags on bags of promo stuff. Welcome to the magical world of baby shopping. It doesn't take your nimble fingers long to acquaint yourself as you pour over catalogue after catalogue of potential purchases that you and your unborn infant apparently can't live without. Nineteen minutes later eighty three tabs are open on the laptop and all of them lead to spending way too much on stuff neither of you really need. Like a custom-made shopping trolley seat cover thingy at €600. A reasonable cost considering it's been lovingly hand crafted by tiny little villagers, in a tiny little town, in a tiny little country mainly populated by balding llamas. Thanks to your purchase you have handsomely contributed to the ***Find a Cure for Balding Llamas Foundation***. Your adoptee is *Drama the Llama*. She has her own Instagram account with 2.9 million followers. You reluctantly check her out. She's a showy bitch.

You move on to some hand-stitched booties only available in a gorgeous little local boutique, which is really just a narrow alleyway suited to those with a more broomsticky physique. It makes for pleasant perusing with one's darling dust brush offspring. You have a gander at their online store. $437.85 and that's just for one booty because apparently pairs are out and *"gorgeous little individuals"* are really *"on point"* right now. You suppress the urge to launch an ear flick to whoever penned the term *on point* and keep surfing.

Million dollar designer clothes are really not a high priority buy, but you need to soothe the retail beast within. There must be something in your booty bags worth clicking *Checkout Now* with abandon?

Your rarely engaged *voice-of-reason* whispers somewhere deep in the cockles. It does try, but you've spent the last three decades ignoring it, so why tune in now? You justify your flippant attitude with the soon to be hammered – *first child* and *first pregnancy* cards. Surely you can splurge a little? You do throwing caution and coin to the wind. Flappity flap.

Green Man has a different stance on the matter of moola and for nine months and wayyyyy beyond will let you know what a waste of money most of your purchases are. You rack up regardless, reminding him of his choice to burrow headfirst into the tequila laced sand rather than join in the baby fun and its prickly financial aftermath. This proves an excellent motivator. Green Man soon cleans himself up just enough to escort you on future outings with a hawk-like eyeball on you and your wallet. He also puts a parent lock on the laptop. Boo. You twirl your phone like a cowboy's pistol and shove it into the holster before Green Man notices smoke coming off. You sensibly decide not to heckle.

Regardless both Mum and bub-to-be need stuff. Time to go shopping.

DO YOU:
A) SHOPPING FOR MATERNITY CLOTHES: PAGE 93
B) SHOPPING FOR BABY: PAGE 43

PAGE 86: WILL THIS BABY EVER COME OUT?

(from page 35)

There may or may not be some discrepancy over whether the due date is correct. You swear it was muffed up right at the beginning, which would make the real due date ten days out! A whopper in the making and your labia puckers at the threat of such stretch!

You plan to plead your case to anyone who will listen. At this point it seems like someone wants to poke, probe and monitor your every minute of the day, so you might as well take advantage and air your concerns. An awkward, pushy preggo reputation won't be an issue as you rarely see the same person twice during these hospital trips.

Since the *Amnio-episode* you've become quite the accommodating patient that draws a few smiles from the poor weary staff. You use your charms and plant the dreaded *induced* seed into every medical encounter, but sadly to no avail. You are still very unsure of what the whole induction thing entails, but from the seventeen second internet search you did in the car seven minutes before your appointment – you feel like a full knowledge bottle on the subject and decide it is just the ticket you need to extract the walrus within. The plan is quickly poo-pooed. Unless you're being admitted as a private patient and have a million dollar obstetrician who is being paid to wholeheartedly believe in your full term twenty-pound scaremongering theories – no one in the public system is interested. You and your healthy, average body and your beautifully healthy, average baby are too normal. Yay… and sod it.

You try your own self-induced mystery tour that turns into self-induced silliness. All theories are up for a crack of cracking the crack and you willingly try most. Spicy foods are first because of course – food. But that gives you heartburn so bad it feels like you're having a curry coronary.

Exercise is next, but walking long distances soon becomes impossible because of the pelvis from hell. There are also concerns you might be mistaken for an escaped zoo animal and accidently tranquilized.

You try the warm bath thing to lure him out, but living in an eighties house built by teeny weeny tiny people means everything is low and pro-gravity. You foresee emergency services bringing in a crane once you swell up like a sponge animal. Bathing is out.

Even your Dad – self-proclaimed doctor of all things medicinally tropical – steps in with his bag full of wives tale tricks. He whips up every pineapple dish he knows because that's apparently what all the preggos did in Mount Isa – a town super well known for its lush, tropical terrain. He serves you up a smorgasbord of BBQ pineapple, cubed pineapple, baked pineapple, pineapple kebabs, pineapple skewers, pineapple mocktail, pineapple with grilled cheese, pineapple ham steaks, pineapple ham steaks with grilled cheese, pineapple upside down cake, pineapple fried rice, pineapple fricassee you thought they only ate in old cartoons, pineapple coleslaw, pineapple frappe, fresh pineapple with a pineapple juice chaser and the list seriously goes on and on and on. To the point where you can't look at the spiky devil fruit for a very long while after. But Tropo MD has more fruit offerings. He goes in on pawpaw next with remedies for rheumatoid arthritis, diabetes, digestion and for the next three hours lists a plethora of benefits for every ailment including bringing on labour – albeit a risky venture. You thankfully miss that last bit of questionable advice and drift away to your own tropical island – pleasantly silent and fruit free.

The self-induced cervix softening efforts continue with everyone jumping on the interweb and sharing their finds. Red raspberry tea is one of the nicer offerings as opposed to castor oil and you call "game-off" when sperm is recommended – to ingest! Green Man's eye widen for a millisecond until he sees your disapproving pucker scowling back at him. He mopes off and takes his sixth shower for the day.

None of it works. No contractions. No labour. No baby exit. Just a laborious count down that never seems to end. You have nightmares of spitting out a wrinkly old man and wake up in a hot sweat. It scares you so badly you give sex a crack and despite Green Man's efforts your bulky let down of errors offers nothing but awkward slapping and not a tickle in sight.

You keep on trucking.

WHAT'S IT TO BE:
A) A DAY OUT: PAGE 18
B) WOMB LOVER: PAGE 11

PAGE 87:
A) RELEASE THE BEASTS

(from page 55)

The fact that this contraption is on wheels and flailing about like a bad fifties robot must mean it's going to hoover the pain with haste. At least you know *this* Midwife is gentle with a lovely bedside manner. An actual bedside manner. With all the madness outside she plows on never tripping on her exhaustion, or taking anything out on you. *This* Midwife is the epitome of professionalism and restores your faith in humans. Even though you've got your gorge game on, you are looking forward to this session and finally getting the hang of your hangers. No more reading, or hearing other's tales. *You* will finally breastfeed your baby with a safe and supportive mentor at your side. You smile in anticipation of the banter the two of you will have as the door re-opens. *Oh no.* This is not the face you were expecting and definitely not the hands you were hoping would guide you on this milestone into Motherhood. It's the *midwitch*. She hovers in and you immediately stiffen.

"The other nurse said she's going to help me," you say confidently in the hopes she will just quietly bugger off. But your voice shakes and all you sense is fear, which of course is ridiculous. Why would a new Mum have anything to fear?

✓ Just about to breastfeed her newborn? Check.

- ✓ Assisted by a midwife trained in all things maternal in a maternity ward? Check.

Put a hold on all things rational for the next few pages. A **lot** of questionable shit is about to go down.

GO TO: PAGE 24

PAGE 88:
A) HOSPITAL CAFETERIA

(from page 75)

You slowly plonk yourself down while Green Man checks out the food options. The hospital cafeteria soon proves to be a breeding ground of other people's happiness and a trigger for your endless supply of sorrow. On top of that some random weirdo is staring at you. Your hypersensitivity makes you immediately paranoid and for good reason.

It's summer, so you have your eighties Mum game on with a light airy dress that supports your leaky, aching bits nicely while still keeping you cool and comfy. Everything is covered up, but apparently not enough for this shitbrick who glares repugnantly at you and your chest. You are incensed knowing full well the type of body hider you actually are.

You've never been a big *get-your-norks-out* kind of chick, though your admiration for friends, family and randoms who display their hooters with pride has always left you envious. It's a level of self-esteem still very foreign to you. Not that you haven't had encouragement. Everyone except you loves your breasts and none more than your family. The big bazookas definitely skipped a few generations and landed firmly on your chest as the women-kin would all help themselves to a grope while oohing, ahhing and gawking at your swingers.

"If you've got 'em flaunt 'em love," they would chant. But you? Just no. Chant-free zone for tyrannosaurus titties. From day dot they were nothing but a back-breaking humiliation for everyone to discuss, stare and point at and by the time you quit competitive sport at the ripe old age of seventeen, they began their droopy descent of no return.

While your Mum could rock out braless tops with her perfect, minuscule mozzie bites – you would deflate at the inflatable and sloppy jugs relentlessly flopping from your chest. The humiliation was never ending. There were few places you could be fitted other than city department stores, normally catering to a more *mature* clientele. The staff would wheel out the bland choices of torture contraptions.

"We call this range the *Boulder Holder* line, dear. Usually only reserved for our fuller figured customers, but it is lovely to see such a young one don them. It's a very practical range," they would chortle gaily. Just what every teenager wants to hear. Not pretty, or lacy, or sexy, or cute – practical. Mint. Much grimacing. Much self-shaming. Much boob-loathing.

"Love every part of yourself," they would also say and you tried. But looking down year after year at what looked like two battered softballs hanging from a pair of sheer stockings – you struggled to find anything lovable about them. A breast reduction has always been on the Christmas list, but Santa never delivers. Damned big-breast-loving tight-arse.

Suffice to say, even when you have completely lost control over the size, direction and capabilities of your feeders – you will still go to great lengths to ensure they are covered up. If for no other reason than you are severely self-conscious about your chest.

However, post-baby you with your engorged triple E's and the freedom that affords you to wear whatever you want without having to check in with anyone – are apparently severely offensive to this cafeteria gawker. You look behind to eliminate any misunderstandings, but there is nothing but a wall. You check that you are covered up *modestly,* and see nothing that could be considered inappropriate. So, you presume you are imagining it and scroll through your phone to ignore him. But, out of the corner of your eye you see him still staring with disgust and he will not look away. Green Man soon returns and sees your distress.

"What's wrong?"

"Nothing."

"What's happened?"

"Nothing. It's okay," you say, but he senses a problem and immediately notices the glaring assclown. You're too exhausted for a scene, but as you look over he eyeballs you with even more disdain – like he actually despises your existence. This is too bizarre to comprehend especially in the state you're in. You just want to be left alone. You try to diffuse it with some limp hypotheticals.

"Maybe I do look a little rough? Or maybe because I don't have bub I've got a bit of a skank on?" You try to make light of it. Which in this type of situation – doing anything other than launching across the tables like a rabid lioness and serving up this man a thunderous mouthful – is strangely out of character for no-putty-up-with-discriminatory-anything you.

"What? You do not and you don't need to justify yourself! You've had a baby," Green Man raises his voice and makes a move. Uh oh. You go to grab his arm, but he's a nimble minx and slips away.

"You right mate?" Green Man is fearless and the glarer suddenly seems very small.

"Sir?"

"Do you have a problem?"

"There is no problem. No problem," the man says. He smiles at Green Man and waves his hands in some sort of erratic peacekeeping motion.

"Can you please stop staring at my wife, or there will be a problem."

"Oh. No... ur... no, sir. There is no problem," says the man again and shakes his limbs vigorously at Green Man who ignores him and walks back to you.

In all the years you've known Green Man he's never once been for alpha wankery and his disinterest fortunately makes him repellant to such nonsense. In fact, it's usually you who causes trouble – mostly because of your intolerance towards unnecessary rudeness and tendency to speak before you think. You run on instincts, usually in defence of others – a decent trait inherited from your equal, open-armed, fair-go-for-all parents. But, right now your instincts are heavily muddled and this chivalrous moment belongs to your husband. You throw him an eye flutter of appreciation. He takes your hand, helps your decrepit self up, and you both exit the café. He glares the entire way at stare-bear man who you thankfully never see again. As you leave you sense a commotion and turn back to see his wife ripping into him. She is unimpressed. She flaps up a serve and wheels her baby out of the cafeteria without him.

"*I am so sorry,*" she mouths to you.

"*It's okay,*" you mouth back, smile and give her the thumbs up. She lowers her head and puts her hands in prayer toward you. You return the gesture. It's a lovely moment from an unnecessary situation and you being a weirdly-unnecessary-situation-magnet are not surprised by any of it. But, you really don't need another issue to overly dissect and let it go.

This hospital is clearly conspiring against you. Time to venture into the suburb you cannot wait to avoid for many, many years to come.

GO TO: PAGE 15

PAGE 89:
B) BACK ROAD

(from page 46)

You take the back roads and drive through at least three major incidents including a car chase, a street festival and finally a booze bus. Green Man has been adorned against his will with shiny necklaces from parade goers and reciprocates the favour by vomiting at every event. One vom near misses a Constable's boot. Thankfully, your belly comes in handy when you start debating with police why you refuse to be breathalysed and nearly break a young officer's hand mid-contraction. They come thick and fast now. The white-knuckled bruising is forgiven and you are not only offered an escort, but they drive you and your car full of winos to the hospital entrance. The night is a successful one for the force as they work until dawn picking up the dodgy loiterers who use a hospital as a local hangout.

Time to get in and get on with it.

GO TO: PAGE 107

PAGE 90:
PART FOUR
DISS-FUNCTION

PAGE 91:
HERE COMES THE BABY

(from page 90)

BUCKLE UP! Seriously. Belt up now! Some high-level madness is about to go down. The baby has certainly chosen a poignant evening to travel down the birth canal and break out into the world. A night of poor life choices, questionable drivers, festive shenanigans and more irrational humans than you can poke an irrational human poking stick at and it's all coming your way!

Get on it.

GO TO: **PAGE 67**

PAGE 92:
B) A LESS RATIONAL APPROACH

(from page 23)

You've been way too calm Chicken Little. Let's check if the sky is falling, shall we? Over the following weeks you ride a tsunami of literature regarding everything ever written about babies, having a baby, being a baby, carrying a baby and the where/what/why/when/how's of being a Mother. You eat, sleep and quite literally shit baby information. It's still very exciting, but super overwhelming. You ingest so many books, blogs and bullshit that some days you wonder if you're going to have a baby, or give birth to an entrepreneurial persona with a healthy social media following and a doctorate in *Balanced-Boss-Babying*. Damn the world has complicated things. Why do all these women look calm? Where is the cellulite? And what is up with *active wear*? The second your brain sees stretchy clothing of any description it goes into fight or flight. Lycra above the knee? Those things can feign a re-vamp, but we all know they're just bike-pants and your butt automatically puckers at the trend that should be vanquished back to 1989.

There are way too many unrealistic expectations going on and the pressure to conform is suffocating especially for non-conformist you. Yet, here you are falling for this really silly and irrelevant crapola. In your defence it's impossible not to. Other people's so-called perfection is everywhere and you watch on as even the most self-loving-power-house women fall victim to this strategic poking at the social conscience. Non-pregnant you would see through the synthetic nonsense of attempting to be anyone other than your glorious self. Sadly, you soon come down with a hard case of *comparisonitis*. You and your oddly changing body don't reflect any of the perfectly sculpted rumps and beautiful sticky-out bumps you keep seeing, mainly on social media. Yours is more of a droopy pancake that seems to wrap its jaloppiness around what was formerly your waist. Like that craze where YouTubers fill a giant balloon with water and jump up and down until it pops and water pisses out everywhere and they all laugh and go back to their thin lives. That's you in permanent slow motion but minus the thin. Never popping. Never releasing the goo. Just herding it to different locations. You sport a more rounded, full-bodied bump, which on most non-hormonal days is not an issue. Nothing matters but your bubby splooshing around enjoying all your delicious cushioning.

Unfortunately, logic has been hijacked and everything you do, see and think of yourself seems heinous. Nothing looks nice, nor does it feel good. You no longer just cater for the land mass out front, but your previously voluptuous booty has taken on a chunk-a-munka life of its own. It's left. It's right. It's round and taut one minute and jellylicious the next. Hipster-goddess garments float off the hangers whispering, *"Be Boho Chic."* Be boho bread and butter pudding more like. Your pre-baby self could barely pull these outfits off and they induce some dangerous flashbacks best left in the archives.

Let's crack one open…

FLASHBACK TIME – CAUTION: TAKE DEEP BREATH

Teenage you was the only size 14 in the very surfie, waif-era village and she dreaded summer in public. Trying on bathers with Mum hanging over the change room door like an insane cheerleader delivering inspirational quotes of love and confidence in a vain attempt at diffusing a severely hostile situation where all you would see was the reflection of an elephant in a bikini and suppress the urge to burn the whole shop and their size fCking 12 and under range to the ground…

... are still some rather raw issues that probably need to be seen to by a professional. Let's just pop the lid back on that potential pandora and take a few steps back. That's the way. Safety first.

While you can ignore every mirror in the house and wash the physical demons down with a bottle of *Lik-Wid-Choc* or two – there are still loads of things to obsessively dissect. Like the uncertainty of your new role as *working Mum* to contend with. A magical universe where career and parenting on your terms co-exist harmoniously. This needling is never far from your thoughts and conjures up a whole lot of unnecessary angst. So, why not get yourself really worked up and dive right into what this future may or may not bring.

Oh, you should totally keep scrolling online too. Scroll, scroll, scroll. It seems to be helping things...

Enjoy that cart ride of calamity.

GO TO: PAGE 54

PAGE 93:
A) MATERNITY SHOPPING

(from page 27 & 85)

You wake up to your bladder's latest chart-topper *BisH-Gotta-PisH* and attempt an actual piss-bolt to the lav. You are much slower than normal and immediately touch your tum. Phew. Still there. Didn't disappear overnight. What has appeared is the DAWN OF THE WADDLE. It is here to stay and it is wayyyy too early.

"Balls to that," you state to no-one and continue on like a rebellious teenager protesting against baby growth and an ever-expanding arse. You peruse your wardrobe, which has apparently developed multiple personalities where the clothes now talk. Yes. Welcome to Dippyland.

SKINNY-JEANS: Do it

DAGGY-BAGGY-TRACKIES: Back in your lane. You're done.

SKINNY-JEANS: Bullshit! Come on, we can squeeze you in! We've done it before!

SLOPPY-JUMPER-WAY-PAST-FASHION-USE-BY-DATE: You're such an attention seeker SJ!

SKINNY-JEANS: Shut your pie-hole old timer! Shouldn't you be crying in a corner somewhere?

SLOPPY-JUMPER: I will take you down, mole!

SKINNY-JEANS: You'll take a hotdog down! We all know she whips you out when it's rag-time.

FAVOURITE-FOOTBALL-FAN-GIRL-SHIRT: Hey guys! Let's support her like a team!

WHOLE-WARDROBE: Shut up, peppy!

SKINNY JEANS: For the record – she would never have conceived if it wasn't for my hustle.

FUR-TRIMMED-COMBAT-COAT: It's a miracle she can ovulate with you crippling her organs on the daily.

SKINNY-JEANS: She lived her best life wearing me!

MISSION-BROWN-NECK-TO-FLOOR-PEASANT-DRESS: She lived her ho life wearing you!

SENSIBLE-WIDE-LEGGED-POWER-CULOTTES: Wearing you? You mean tattooing you.

SKINNY-JEANS: Ignore them. This baby won't change us!

JEGGINGS: Move over bishes! It's lycra time!

SKINNY-JEANS: NEVER!

You grab the skinny-jeans, pause a moment, then grab the jeggings just in case. No point doing two trips. Plonking yourself on the bed, you commence proceedings. You catch yourself in the mirror and despair at the shit you have to pull just to be clothed. You are one face mask and a rubber glove away from a surgical procedure. The bed feels a lot higher than normal and you struggle to reach your ankles like the bendy days of a month ago. You haul yourself into the middle of the bed using gravity to your advantage, but even the most basic of scientific laws has abandoned your escapades and you lie panting with barely half a denim leg pulled up your calf.

"Bullshit," you yell again to the air. You reach for the jeggings that slip on with devastating ease. Back to the wardrobe you survey the choices and come to the only realistic option. The oversized jumper dragged through the decades that never let you down during your heavier moments. It pairs wonderfully with the roomy lycra.

JEGGINGS: All hail my stretching capabilities! Kiss it SJ!

SKINNY-JEANS: Shove it up your fake arse!

JEGGINGS: Oh, I am all over that arse!

SKINNY-JEANS: Are you seriously flipping the bird Sloppy Jumper?

SLOPPY-JUMPER: Oath! I'm mainstream again… not that I give a shit.

SKINNY-JEANS: Try not to disintegrate once the sunlight hits you.

JEGGINGS: Enjoy the back of the wardrobe has-been!

The psychotic-inner-clothing-monologue has a point you can no longer deny. It's time to shop for more appropriate Mother-to-be attire. You can't keep running around like you're off clubbing with your fly undone and half a gut roll hanging out. Problem is you have no idea where to buy maternity clothes and realise how different your priorities have become. The only time you've paid the slightest attention to *watermelon* wear was many pre-baby years ago. You mistakenly tried on a maternity dress and was horrified that it not only fit, but looked good! Unfortunately, you can't remember what store it was from. So you rummage through the goodie bags collected at the baby e**X**po and fish out the four billion cards thrust at you amidst the madness.

Eventually you figure things out even if the lessons burn a small hole in your wallet. Shopping for maternity clothes at high-end stores specifically marketing to preggos – is for high-end preggos. Good on them if they can afford it. You have nothing against financially successful slayers. But, you do struggle to justify the EXORBITANT prices being asked for an item you will most likely wear a few months, ruin with stains and stretching so extreme that even the charity bin would raise an eyebrow. Plus, that's a lot of chocolate bullets and triple zero onesies you could buy instead. You finally remember where you tried the dress and head on over. You soon discover that leggings and maxi-anything are to become your best friends and thank the fertility gods you are spending the heavier end of your pregnancy during winter. You stock up and load up kissing the mortified cashier when she announces the cost of your haul is nearly 70% less than what you paid for one item at the high-end store. You pat your growing girth contently, make a note to hug a yuppie next time you see one in the wild and forget it twenty five seconds later.

All this closet banter tuckered you out. Grab a cuppa. It's time to start the *Birth Plan*.

GO TO: PAGE 56

PAGE 94:
A) FRESH GODDESS

(...BABY GIRL JOURNEY CONTINUED)

(from pages 16, 51 & 114)

Y ou freshen up and paint your nails Bollywood Pink. You feel fantastic afterwards with no niggling pain and bub seems to have relaxed. You give her a gentle shove just to be sure and receive a delightful little limb protrusion from what used to be your navel. Lovely. Birds are singing and you feel like a goddess. In fact, you are a damn embodiment of Gaia! One with the earth! An ethereal vessel with a waddling swagger. You sit poignantly on a sturdy, weight bearing chair Green Man secretly reinforced with a thick piece of factory grade, industrial strength steel. You ponder Motherhood and how you will most likely slay. Actually, that could very well be your child's middle name.

Bonzai Scarlett 'Slay' Man.

Catchy. You make a note to share this inspirational nugget with Green Man and forget it six seconds later as he appears at the door.

"Are you ready babe?"

Yes. You are.

It's time to meet your little girl.

GO TO: PAGE 70

PAGE 95: PRE-NATAL CLASSES

(from page 17)

You are so excited to go to *Lamaze* classes because you just want to say *Lamaze* over and over like they do in the movies, because of course it's all going to be exactly like that. Shocker – it's not. It's all very anti-natal no-nonsense stuff that you struggle to stay focused on.

The whole experience proves to be a bit full on for Green Man too, highlighting yet again his delusional denial. He can't drink his way through this one, so he takes the mature path of coping via humour. Really woefully, inappropriate humour. It's nothing these midwives haven't heard before, but he thinks his sick cliché jokes are hilarious and uses the opportunity as a stand-up routine that no one particularly wants to hear. He busies himself cracking gags about hairy muffs and hippie porn nearly getting you thrown out several times.

HIM: You'd think they'd update the video?

YOU: Pretty sure giving birth is un-updateable. Not much has changed.

HIM: Fashion has. That guy looks like the 1978 Australian cricket team and the lady giving birth... well... whoa.

YOU: Why does everything turn into a porno with you?

HIM: Trust me. This is anti-horn.

YOU: Just shush and watch. What are you doing to that doll?

HIM: One-handed push-up.

YOU: Leave it alone. Concentrate.

HIM: I am. Hand me your jumper.

YOU: Why?

HIM: Look. Bandana baby!

YOU: Seriously?

HIM: One more…

YOU: No!

HIM: Super gangster baby! He's got a durag!

You snatch your cardigan and wrap it around your waste. Green Man pouts. Even though his material *is* quite funny, it's of no use to your brain that is currently retaining information like an abandoned sieve. So you employ the aid of your beautiful, supportive Aunty who is a walking info vacuum and thrives in this environment like a butterfly. It's a lovely bonding time for you both. One of the original IVF pioneers – she went through the labour ordeal four times and glows in this space. She is in her element, loving every second of all things birthy. She fits in perfectly, like a thumb in a bum. You are grateful she's here because quite frankly GM is like tits on a bull, or so that's what he appears to be.

On the final night everyone mingles and swaps emails to create a Mothers' group after the babies are born. You get talking with a few of the other Mums-to-be and notice the lack of pain-relief chatter – a topic you haven't shut up about since the two pink lines. There is much flowery nattering about *natural* and *fitball* and *water-birthing* and other non-drug talk. You slip "epidural" into a conversation and the whole room goes silent. Suddenly it feels like everyone is surrounding you and they may or may not be wearing dystopian attire. One of the Midwives makes a beeline for you. She's cloaked... okay she's not. Everyone is dressed normally, but a heaviness fills the air and you feel like you're on trial.

"We only offer gas at the PRIMAL WOMB HOUSE dear. You were aware of this when you applied, surely?" the Midwife questions. Her tone sounds shocked and a little irritated by your ignorance at this late stage. Green Man smirks. He knows the magical gift you possess of completely missing major chunks of important information on an alarmingly frequent basis. This gift has increased to mung bean heights since falling pregnant and it's a miracle you know how to form sentences. You throw him a death stare and he lovingly puts a protective arm around you.

"I kept telling you this was the hippie section," he whispers and even though you want to lovingly give him an uppercut to his correctly informed moushe, you refrain and curse your mudpie brain for failing again.

"But I can get an epidural if I need it? Right? In an emergency?"

"You can if you want one dear, but not here," she responds sounding disappointed, like she's just lost one of the flock. She lowers her head and points to the fortress of doom on the hill. It looks like a former asylum from a lawless era and there is an actual storm cloud hovering. The room simultaneously shudders at the sight of it, but none more than you.

Oh.

FCk.

DO YOU:
A) PACK UP YOUR SHIT AND LEAVE: PAGE 99
B) PULL UP YOUR BIG GIRL PANTS: PAGE 40

PAGE 96:
A) GO TO LUNCH

(from page 52)

Beautiful Bestie with her beautiful beastie take you to a quirky little cafe she knows will perk you up. It's got lots of pregnant friendly options and the whole thing is covered with books. You take it all in and hug her tight. She is just a mint-julip friend who knows you so well. You feel very hashtag blessed to have such great mates and hope you won't drain them dry in the coming weeks, months, years, decades.

You enjoy the meal, squeeze little howler's bub-chub and share a tonne of laughs. You say your farewells and feel positive about things again until the drive home where you spiral into *Doubtsville* once more. You try to keep the impending gloom from your mind, but the task seems hopeless. Your cup that usually overflows has become empty and numb.

There's no getting around what's to come.

GO TO: PAGE 101

PAGE 97:
B) BUZZ FOR ASSISTANCE

(from page 2 & 60)

Coleslaw was apparently the salad of choice tonight and the entire ward is going off! Old wives' tale or not, it seems the theory on cabbage → converted to → breast milk = screaming little infant tummies – is proving correct this eve. The sounds of buzzers and babies in pain echo down the hallway walls accompanied by the frantic footsteps of staff under the pump.

You've nervously procrastinated over your own request for assistance and finally push your thumb down on the button. It takes forever for someone to respond and unfortunately for you the only staff who reluctantly comes to your aid is the midwife from hell – forever known as the *midwitch*. Without looking at you she goes straight to bub who you had to push away because of the freezing breeze hammering down on him. She checks the chart, mumbles and eventually acknowledges you in an odd manner.

"Are you in pain? The spinal block has probably worn off. I'll get some relief."

"Yes, thank you. Could you please help me to the bathroom so I can have a shower? And I don't mean to be annoying, but is there any chance I can get some new sheets and the bed be moved away from the vent?"

"Don't worry about all that. You can have a shower in the morning and there's nothing wrong with the bedding," she snaps as if annoyed you have the gall to make requests, let alone speak. **Wrong answer.** You are cold, in pain and exhausted and figure you are entitled to ask of these basic rights after giving birth and waiting alone for nearly five hours. With what little energy you have remaining you throw back the bed covers to reveal the blood-soaked mess. It looks far worse than it felt. The hospital gown is saturated from your calves to your chest. The blood has long dried and sticks to your wounds. The pooling at your sides is still deep, though it too has coagulated into clotty bits of gooey wrongness. Tears well. The *midwitch* gasps and then quickly recovers. You don't give her a chance to speak.

"Surely you don't expect me to sleep in this? I haven't been cleaned from having my son. I need a shower now. Can you help me? Please," you plead, frustrated you have to.

"All right," is all she says. You sense a shift in her attitude. It's not sympathy – more a validation for why she needs to stay and do her actual job. You feel like a shitty inconvenience and in the coming days will pay for the outburst. For now you could care less and are oblivious to the soon to be understood wrath of the *midwitch*.

She helps you to the shower and offers to come in. You decline, abruptly closing the door. Everything is awkward. Everything hurts. Trying to get undressed attached to a drip is hard enough, but because of the dried blood situation, as you peel off the garment it yanks at the skin adding another layer of pain. Thankfully, when the hot water hits it washes most of the goo and trauma temporarily down the plughole. Ironically, the shortest shower you will ever take will also be the most wonderful.

You ask the *midwitch* to pass your toiletries and the nightie you were so excited packing. You look at your reflection and recall the naïve anticipation you had for this life-changing moment that has turned rather sour. You cry, but only briefly. You don't want her to see. You brush your teeth and hair and feel a bit more human.

When you come out the bed has been re-made and repositioned. *midwitch* helps you back into the fresh sheets, hands you bub and turns to leave.

"Your next lot of pain killers will be at 3:30. Buzz if the baby needs a feed," is all she offers and walks out. After the highest heights in a room full of loved ones and medical staff who were all championing your success, you are again alone and deflated. But, you are clean and warm and grateful for that. You put bub back into the crib and pull it close.

"You are all that matters," you whisper and with your lovely lumpy infant cooing softly with his little hand wrapped around your finger, you fall asleep, in love.

What seems like seconds later you are wrenched from a death-like slumber. Your maternal instincts kick in with full force – something you will later appreciate when that intuition upgrades to superhero status. Mother Nature's way of helping to decipher when things are not right with your kids. Combined, these gifts come in handy when solving life's deep problems like – which of your darling offspring left an unflushed turd in the toilet? Or who really did steal the last cookie from the cookie jar? Who me? Probably. Unfortunately, those intuitive gifts will be tested in ways that will be mentally draining for you and your infant over the following weeks.

The abrupt wake-up call consists of pain and a hand in the dark holding a cupful of drugs to your face. You happily slug them back without question and frantically reach out to make sure your son is still there. He is. The door slams and you cross your fingers it was *midwitch*'s final shift before a long, long service leave to an isolated country far, far away.

Yeah, na. You really should know at this point that luck is not your pal what-so-ever. Like, not remotely. At all. Don't even bother chasing. Instead, get ready for one of those sucky life lessony/resilience building thingies necessary to write a book in the hopes that women suffering any type of aftermathy madness will know they're not alone and will do the total opposite.

GO TO: PAGE 30

PAGE 98:
B) YOUR OVERPRICED WELLBEING

(from page 47)

Splishity splash it's raining cash. Private it is. Good news – you've somehow jagged the easiest going obstetrician to ever walk the earth. He barely speaks, only probes your belly every other month, never once asks to see your nethers until the finale and enjoys your sarcastic, witty banter that grows more brutally inappropriate with every daily discomfort. He is a dream for anti-social, no touchy, no talky, no time wasty – you.

You can forgive the fact that you have to pay ridiculous fees for parking and waddle your landmass an extended distance with a bladder brimful of urine. You can even forget the rubfest your tubness attracts. As this is a general hospital you are apparently open season to every walk of life who sporadically enjoy rubbing a baby belly. They rub in the elevator. They rub in line for the ticket machine. They rub in the ladies lav. They rub when you're just sitting like a quiet rub-free, business-minding hippopotamus. They rub away as if pellets are going to pop out and everyone can feed the farm animals. However, the perks of this place are worth the rubs. Waiting times are minimal and there are so many conveniences it's like a damned shopping centre. Plus, Jesus smiles down from every conceivable surface as if to say,

"Good choice child. Forgeteth the final bill-eth. Thou shalt dealeth with on a day fareth, fareth away... eth."

Cheers Jeshua. You throw the original hipster a wink and take up the good word – *blessed be thy fruit* – and mow down a banana. At the end of the day that baby is still coming out and no matter what bed of denomination your arse is lying on – things are going to get messy.

GO TO: PAGE 44

PAGE 99:
A) PACK UP YOUR SHIT

(from page 95)

Since your earliest comprehension of the spoken word you have been told what a ten-tonne heifer you were to give birth to. A total watermelon. The hefty experience was enough for your mother to never go back for seconds. So, you reason that the likelihood of your baby being smaller than a grizzly bear is slim and it will be a hard sell to convince you otherwise. There is no way you are doing this with a toke of gas and a flipping fitball!

The mortified group awaits as you quickly nod and laugh convincingly at your supposed faux pas.

"Ha ha! Brain fart! Epidural? As if," you offer unconvincingly as everybody chortles gaily and there are well wishes all round. You play along, quietly planning your chicken-shit intentions. You don't care anymore. You will most likely be banished from the PRIMAL WOMBERS Mothers' group anyway and hence will never see any of these *Super Utereo* heroes ever again. C'est la vie.

"Catch ya later ladies," you call and imagine a frollicking sunset scene where your throbbing-pain-blocking-syringy-lover gently lowers you to the sand and gives you a right royal poking into your bare skinned spine. Rowrlll!

Once the epidural porn dissipates you feel like a wussy ding-a-ling for bailing out of the *titanium-sabre-labia-club*. You ring your friend who recently went through the PRIMAL WOMB HOUSE experience and pepper her with questions in the hopes she can soothe your guilt with a horror story. She does. Hers was a forty-hour labour where she was taken to the main hospital anyway to have a life-saving caesarean. The recovery for Mum and baby girl – was a long one, both physically and mentally. The experience turns her off having children forever. It isn't until a decade later when a happy accident gives her a second chance to experience the joys of giving birth without the horror attached. Isolated incident or not it's enough to completely scare the shit out of your drug-free intentions and seals you up good and tight.

The problem now is getting into another hospital this late in the game. She advises you to play the *age* card. You are a staggering thirty four years and close to the supposedly high-risk portion of life where your decrepit reproductive system can apparently pack it in at any second. You shelve the ageism protest and begin hatching a plan based on the thing that has dogged you forever. Your size. *Big babies = Big pain.* Hopefully, some sympathetic soul will wave your big old body into the loving arms of a steady-handed inducing enthusiast. You are one hairless cat and a hidden lair from bringing it all to fruition and tomorrow the big baby campaign begins. Mwa-ha-ha.

All evil geniuses need a sneaky snack. You mow into a doughnut, two bananas, a pregnancy protein bar, Green Man's mandatory smoothie, a bag of bullets and wash the lot down with half a bottle of *Lik-Wid-Choc* before calling it a night.

Good gravy woman! There'll be no room left for the baby soon!

GO TO: PAGE 45

PAGE 100:
A) ZOMBIE APOCALYPSE POSTAL

(from page 77)

What a treat! Thanks to *Superdick* you can experience one of your all-time favourite genres. Later that night the phone rings. It's Nan.

NAN: Hi love.

YOU: Hi Nan.

NAN: Just checking you're okay. I heard what happened.

YOU: What happened?

NAN: Don't you know? At your hospital there was some sort of strange attack!

YOU: Really?

NAN: Yes! It's been all over the telly. They said a group of women sucked a man dry. Guzzled the life out of him. Like zombies!

YOU: No!

NAN: Yes! They said for the sake of humanity he had to go. They called him something… What was it they called him? I wrote it down in me little pad here… hang on a sec.

YOU: *Superdick*, Nan?

NAN: Oh, I wish you wouldn't use that language love, you know I don't… oh… yes. You clever thing. Got it right here in me little pad. *SU-PA-DICK*.

YOU: He probably deserved it, Nan.

NAN: Yes, well nobody likes a clever clogs.

YOU: True dat, Nan. True dat.

You hang up the phone, pick a bit of gristle from a molar and pat your full tum. Should make for some nutrient rich breast milk.

Let us leave the daydreams of cannibalism here shall we and head back to a less psychotic approach of dealing with our frustrations. Off you trot.

GO TO: PAGE 73

PAGE 101: WAITING FOR RESULTS

(from page 96 & 36)

Everything you've filled your brain with of late seems so trivial as an overwhelming heaviness sets in. It's not your way to see the cup as anything but half full, and as Mum always says, *"There's a solution to every problem, darl."* Onya Mum ♥

Unfortunately, it appears your hormones are running the show and you feel powerless and hopeless. The not-knowing is hard enough. It's the waiting that does your head in. For two weeks you occupy an uncertain space filled with angst-fueled sorrow for things that may or may not happen. Not only do you not know if your little sprout will pull through, but there are conversations you and Green Man should be having that neither of you can entertain. So he hugs you and brings broth and chocolate because he has no idea how to deal with any of it. Neither do you.

You've been sent home from work because of sporadic breakdowns. Probably for the best to clear your head. You set up camp on the couch and cry and knit and stare at screens. You cry some more and no amount of knitting, woeful day time TV watching, internet fear-mongering, or chatting to very well-meaning family and friends can stop the relentless amount of tears that continue to come. It feels like this will be your sorrowful reality forever even though somewhere amidst all this silliness you know it's not permanent.

You cry yourself into a restless sleep each night consumed by every scenario of the worse possible outcomes. You know you're being over the top, but no one can tell you for certain if your baby, or you are low risk for any of it, or if any of those worse case scenarios are officially off the table.

GREEN MAN: This is a piss-take.

YOU: What is?

GREEN MAN: Putting hormonally imbalanced women through this bullshit. You'd think the tech would be more advanced at this point, surely?

YOU: I love how you geek-out in any situation.

GREEN MAN: Inefficiency shits me.

You were keen for Green Man to get more involved, but not like this. He later admits the feelings of powerlessness were overwhelming for him too, something he never wanted either of you to experience again.

Finally, you are both put out of your misery when you get the call. It's the technician herself who is so concerned about your wellbeing, she rings in person. The baby is fine. In fact, everything about you, your baby and your pregnancy are normal. She justifies the whole ordeal as "precautionary measures" and while you truly do appreciate and are sincerely grateful to live in a society where you are privileged to have a medical system that will run complicated tests just to eliminate every risk factor that they can – *precautionary measures* will be a term you come to despise long after your baby is born.

For now, you thank her profusely through a flood of tears which finally are joy-filled. You ring Green Man, family and friends who are all relieved and send you oceans of love. Out of the woods you are determined to avoid anything resembling those depths of despair again. You swipe away the tears, plump out your butt mould in the couch and rejoin society.

Give yourself a huge hug. It may not have been ideal, but you and bubbikins have made it to three months. Now go enjoy the second trimester. Home of *the glow*, easy movement, still seeing your bits and peeing with frustrating frequency.

END OF THE FIRST TRIMESTER

GO TO: PAGE 32

PAGE 102:
A) GREEN MAN'S WELLBEING

(from page 47)

Alas this is not to be your fate. Besides, you'll probably need that cash to fund the baby shower purchases you've been racking up. After the shitnado you're about to go through, Green Man boldly states he will personally book you into the private hospital himself for the next pregnancy. You don't forget and twirl your imaginary beard hair between your fingers. Mwa ha ha.

GO BACK: PAGE 106

PAGE 103:
B) CALL A TAXI

(from page 67)

Your sad excuse of a *support group* has fallen back to sleep, so you call a taxi, which this close to Christmas is like calling a rocket to Mars. You grab a faded charter card off the fridge and cross your fingers they're still operating. They are. Yay, but there's only one vehicle left. Oh. Who happens to be in the area. Yay again. But, it's not a car. Okay? It's a limo and as the driver nears he sees how far gone you are and puts pedal to the discriminatory metal. You watch him poorly pretending he doesn't actually see the obvious vision you are on the side of the road in the middle of the night in bloody labour! Whatever. You get it. Who wants any of that cray-cray on their leather interior during the business booming silly season. Still – rude.

Just as you prepare to yell a string of abuse he pulls into your neighbour's house and the perky, flat stomached, non-leaking teenagers pile in. You suddenly feel the urge to throw cartons of condoms and Mum quips at them.

"Make good choices! Your yoni ain't a jar of honey!"

Thankfully you don't and slowly wade back inside. Even though the limo wasn't yours, you vouch a vendetta against all people moving services and forget it before the vengeance even makes it to your cerebral cortex. That thing packed its bags and left ages ago. Nothing but rock bongos in there now. It may be grunty, but it's a good rhythm.

GO TO: PAGE 46

PAGE 104:
B) THE SHOWER/ SHAVE DILEMMA

(...BABY BOY JOURNEY CONTINUED)

(from page 29 & 51)

You manage to undress and somehow pour your body into the shower. Unlike squeezing toothpaste back into the tube – this is the equivalent of trying to do it with honey-glazed ham legs for hands. You attempt to *tidy-up*. Oh, how you try. But your big arse baby bump is hanging so low – nothing is getting near that region.

You try a mirror. You drop the mirror. Don't worry it doesn't break. The reflection of your Medusa nethers hardened it like titanium and it's little more than a stone version of itself now. You have a quick squiz and scar a retina. As predicted it's a nightmare down there. It would be a miracle if this baby doesn't take one look and claw its way back up your rib cage rather than risk hacking through that thorny forest of doom.

You reassess the shave options. Maybe you can get creative with a chair? Throw a leg up or something? But you'll need the mirror. Back to the mirror? Seriously, forget it. It's no longer an option. RIP the mirror!

You consider paying a professional, but foresee several issues. With the amount of wax they're going to need to make a dent in your lady fro there's a high probability of wiping the planet's bee population. You know once the bees are gone you and your jungers are royally fCked and who wants to bring a baby into a bee-less, hairy world like that?

Au naturel it is. Don't stress. Embrace your seventies-porn-parade and waddle free! You do exactly that and at your moment of liberation Green Man walks in mid-embracement and turns a pale shade of *what-the-holy-hell?* You say nothing and smile. He no longer has the ability to form sentences and evaporates back out the door in a ghost cloud. You put your hands on your hips and start singing songs of empowerment and long beautiful hair. One song mentions a candle, which reignites the whole waxing saga, that gets you thinking about bees again, that leads to thoughts of honey, which reminds you it's been at least sixteen minutes since you last ate.

Time to get your glutton-groove on. Head on down to mow town.

Nom.

Nom.

Nom.

GO TO: PAGE 17
OR
IF YOU HAVE ALREADY STUFFED YOURSELF
GO TO: PAGE 41

PAGE 105:
B) THE FREEWAY

(from page 46)

The freeway was a good choice. Smooth, straight and anti-vomit inducing for poor ole Green Man who will hopefully sleep it off. He doesn't and on top of his hideous drunken stupor he suffers car sickness too. You keep looking back and reaching for his leg.

"Oh, babe. Are you okay?"

"He's fine. Just watch the road, young lady," your Mum intervenes and holds her hand over your tum like it's a turkey that's about to drop out of the oven.

"He's spewing out the window, Mum. He might have alcohol poisoning."

"Well, he'll be in good hands then."

"In the maternity ward?"

"He'll be fine. Eyes on the road."

"Mum. There is no one around. I've got four lanes to myself and I'm going seventy five kilometres!"

"What? At least do the speed limit!"

"I just thought I should go slow being in labour and all!"

"Stop being dramatic. How long since your last contraction?"

"Um… about four… min… utes… here's ano… ther… one…!"

"Put your foot down, love! I won't have my Grandson born on the freeway."

"Yes… of course… because your daugh… ter… can't wait to give birth in a car!!"

"Bull… shhiiit! Emergency… lane! You can sssit on the… curb…ussse… the… tow… el!" Green Man heaves and though it's hard to take him seriously through all the dry-retching, you know he means every word. The evening is clear, warm and the views are lovely, despite the violent sounds of your husband spewing repeatedly out the window. He regurgitates half of what flies back into his mouth and still gives an unnatural shit about the car.

"Make sssure you… w…wa…washh it off sso… doesssn't… ssstrip the paint!!"

"Just spew quietly, *you*. She needs to concentrate!" your Mum yells back. She's over it. Green Man passes out again. The prospect of having your baby with bits of gravel digging into your arse cheeks is incentive enough to put your foot down. You get the deed done so well that you never know how you made it to the front of the hospital. Probably not a bad thing. On the plus side having babies in the wee hours of the morn means plenty of parking and no need to drive right up to the front doors. The only thing stopping you is a woman holding onto a drip (attached) sucking down a cigarette who probably wouldn't appreciate being hit mid-drag by your venga bus. She lives to see another day as you jag a park right at the front. Mum helps you out and collects your stuff. You waddle forth with Green Man who suddenly wraps his arm tight around your waist. You kiss him on his disgustingly clammy cheek, flick a bit of miscellaneous vom from his beard and smile. Whether he is supporting or leaning on you is questionable, but there's no time to ponder as drip lady now shuffles towards you both.

"Aaahhh the Mumma to be," she booms. Turns out she's neither crazy, nor scary just really friendly and a fan of pregnant women who drive themselves to give birth. She wears the most amazing scarlet lipstick and has a deliciously thick accent. Even though the pain is getting harder to ignore, you can't help but take a moment to stare at this random greeter. She glows and if there was no metal pole or hospital gown, you'd swear she was off for a night on the town.

"I see you driving yourself to give baby! Yes! What a woman," she booms again. She lops her spare arm over yours and escorts you to the doors. The clattering of the IV stand echoes throughout the silent streets. Green Man holds his flank pulling you a little closer to him. His paranoia amuses your peace, love and serial-killer-free vibe right now. You wonder – what possible threat could this woman *really* be capable of?

"Oh, thank you. It wasn't that bad," you offer and rest your hand on hers.

"No! Embrace this, dear girl!" she insists.

"It's no big deal. I'm sure women have gone through way worse things."

"Yes, but you must own it. Tell the world this story," she cries out lifting her head to the heavens.

"Okay. Maybe someday," you reply between giggles.

"Go now! Have your baby!"

"Thank you and you take care too."

"Look after your Queen, drunk man," she yells to Green Man who nods, his grip around your waist so tight it feels like a hostage situation.

"What are you worrying about? She's cool."

"You're in labourrr with no... no... onnne around and I amm... like a tt... tttt... tad... pole. Less go."

"I think she's amazing. What a welcome!"

"I'm shoorrre the hopsipal did it... juss for usss. Wasss ssheee even pregnann?"

Another contraction reminds you why you're here. You shrug your shoulders and as hard as you try none of you will ever recall if the woman looked as if she had given birth, or was in the midst of doing so. You smile whenever you think of her. She was cool-as.

BUT – now the time has finally come to limber up your slippery dip.

GO TO: PAGE 107

PAGE 106:
A) PUBLIC HOSPITAL

(from page 21 & 102)

A dear colleague has told you about the lovely PRIMAL WOMB HOUSE option. It sounds very calm, sensitive, sensible and completely opposite to your personality traits. You attend one of their tours to investigate further. It's impressive.

All the Midwives are friendly and have a sense of humour you can relate to. The rooms are homely and set up so that half the country can attend your literal crowning glory. You are in such an elated state that this baby joy is finally happening and gleefully sign up with barely a question asked. Green Man comes-to briefly from his zombified coma and watches on as you fill out the forms and are booked into the primal-baby-birthy-club. You later learn to appreciate how much that man can take in *and* retain even when he looks like he should be hooked up to a life-support for perpetually hungover gluttons. He knew the end outcome of the PRIMAL WOMB HOUSE:

NO EPIDURAL

He even tries to bring it up with you, but the combination of your elation and his brewery stenched gob kicks in your inner all-knowing, irritated teen. You stupidly ignore his council. He shrugs his shoulders in an *Oh well. I barely tried. She'll find out eventually* way and lets it go. **THAT** he lets go. Of all the things you wish he had piped up about over the coming months – **THAT** bit of info would have been better shared. You will never understand why he didn't enlighten your clearly frazzled brain and boy how frazzled it must have been. Even a non-birther with absolutely zilcho interest in having a baby would have worked it out quicker than you. There was SO much paraphernalia promoting all things *primal-and-one-with-the-drug-free-womb* – even your baby probably noticed. Not you. Fool.

Many, many years later you would find yourself blessed to be a part of a beautiful community who master in bringing babies earthside in a loving, nurturing and soul-nourishing manner for all involved. You'll dance and sing and break bread with many of these women. You'll meet beautiful Doulas and will envy their birthing tales and even their child rearing ways. Ways that seemed so unreal to you, wisdom of long ago when females followed their natural flow, embracing the process in its entirety – the beauty and raw grit of bringing a child into the world.

Pregnant, un-awakened, 21st century you, however, would rather skip the warrior woman stuff for a delightful hit of pure modern day spinal blockage. Something you won't be getting here. When the time comes for you to beg for relief, you'll be offered some paracetamol, a heat pack, gas that makes you vomit and a fCking fitball.

Oh dear, delusional hippie girl. What have you done?

GO TO: PAGE 43

PAGE 107:
TIME TO GIVE BIRTH

(from page 89 & 105)

It feels like you've arrived at the airport and are being checked for drug smuggling. You all wait in some sort of holding room where you change into a gown that will remain on long after you have your child. The contractions come quicker, though not quick enough to warrant immediate entry into the birth wards.

"Hang in there, dear," a Midwife calls out. She gently helps you into the gown.

"Would you like a fitball?" another offers as she records notes onto a clipboard that will follow you right up until you actually need them.

"What? Why?"

"It helps relieve the pressure."

"The pressure means he's coming out right? No, thank you," you curtly reply, though it won't be the last of the fitball talk.

The Midwives finish their fossicking and hover near your curtained cubicle. You grab the side of the mattress as another wave comes.

One sticks her head back in like an overzealous ostrich. "How about some paracetamol?"

"Is she kidding?" you throw the query to Mother Sophia who pats your arm gently in her *just keep your cool* Mum-manner.

"I can get you a heat pack?" the Midwife says through a giggle.

"No, seriously. Is this a joke?" you question a bit too abruptly. You just want to know where the epidural is at and Mum nudges you like she can read your mind. In labour or not – she rarely tolerates rudeness. But, those happy hormones that had you cleaning up spew and fluttering around like the fairy bread princess of lollypop land – have officially gone. You have minimal care factor for polite protocols. The pain is here and you'd like to kick the main element of the *Birth Plan* into gear before you kick someone in the head. You did not abandon the PRIMAL WOMB HOUSE to be denied the one reason you jumped ship in the first place!

The Midwives smile, knowingly. You can only imagine the insane crap they must see hourly and you feel like a piney brat for the outburst. It's a redundant dummy spit anyway. Unbeknownst to you is the madness occurring next door. An anaesthetist runs like a madman up and down a ward choc-a-block full of women in wayyyy more pain and reason to complain. No wonder the Midwives snicker. They smile sympathetically knowing your spine is in for a long, long, long wait before it will be serviced. Another wave hits.

"Not long now, love. You're going to do well. Just breathe," says fitball Midwife who rubs your back reassuringly. You appreciate the generous lie and are grateful for the empathy. You breathe deeply, nod agreeably and take up the offer of a heat pack. She bounces off enthusiastically. It will be hours before you see it as you are soon wheeled into the main ward. They are ready for you.

The stark quiet of the holding room is soon replaced by clankering bustle and women in pain. You clench and recall nervous squeezing is no longer an option. Your sorry crew trail behind and seem super alert. Tears brew and considering nothing has really happened yet, you're embarrassed to release them. The fear churns and you sense a panic attack lurking. The bed hoons along the fluorescent white corridor before being thrust into a room where two of the kindest-looking women patiently await you. They glow like magical multi-tasking unicorns who immediately start to fuss and roll and prod and fold and pat and write and press and pull. They dance around like graceful swans and their only focus is the sphere occupied by you.

"Evenin', Mrs Man. I'm Brighid and this is Juliette. We'll be taking care of you," Brighid speaks as she fusses. They remind you of those ladies handing out free food in shopping centres – too good to be true. These two are just as smiley as the petty-pain-relieving-fitball-pushing-peddlers you just left and you wonder if everyone around here is taking a cheeky hit from the entonox bong.

Brighid happily chatters as you watch her dart about. She has a thick Scottish accent which you barely understand, but somehow comprehend every single instruction she gives, including her intolerance for sooks.

"I won't have soppiness in my ward. Now come on, be brave," she orders and you snot laugh. She gently wipes away your tears and you have never been so keen to please.

The other angel – Juliette is literally straight from a Shakespearean romance and has an approach so sweet she's like fairy floss with limbs. She pats down your clammy brow and strokes your hair while you go in and out of consciousness. She is a trainee and you are the final birth that will conclude her Midwifery studies. You feel honoured your baby will give her a pass and are grateful to share such a prestigious moment. You hope you don't fCk it up.

A few hours later your Aunty arrives to complete the merriest suite in the hospital. The room is filled with love and joy and there is way more laughter than there probably should be.

The hours pass, the pain increases and your one request of a juicy squirt of relief has still not been granted. A tonne of emergency caesareans have come through and the anaesthetist is running up and down the corridor like a puppy chasing a cupcake on a seesaw. The

Midwives wipe your forehead and rub your arm soothingly. Neither you, nor the baby are in any danger and are pushed down the epidural list. There's nothing to do, but deal with it. They offer you gas which makes you vomit, so they try their best to source every tool in their Midwifery kit to relieve you of both pain and the baby who refuses to budge.

"Would you like to go onto your hands and knees, lovey?"

"Doggy style?"

"I wager it's probably doggy style that got you in here," Brighid jokes. *Bring in the mic! We have a comedian in birth suite 14!* She cackles loudly and everyone laughs except you. Green Man dares to twirl his finger and you glare up a fireball.

"Whooppp... whoop," he mumbles between hiccups.

"I will break that finger and shove it where the *whoop whoop* goes to die, mate," you whisper icily and the room is in hysterics.

"Oooh, look out. We've got a live one here!" Brighid opens the door and yells to the corridor and it seems that in no time the entire ward knows of Viper-Veruca and her drunken golden goose. You, however, can't get over the doggy-style suggestion. Did no-one read the birth plan? Who knows where that useless fCker has gone, but it's clearly not here. Boo. You can't believe you are giving in to *all-fours*. It doesn't last long. As predicted the position is awkward, heavy and feels more painful than before. Your knees take pity and crack so loudly everyone helps you back over like a crumbly sausage roll.

"How about a fitball, darlin'?" the Scottish Queen asks as you suppress a scowl. What is up with the fitball? Why do people keep peddling this plastic arsehole? The words *fit* and *childbirth* sound very anit-matchy for very anti-fit you. You don't want to offend the women charged with assisting your firstborn into the world, so you aim your snarling death stare at one of the few people in the room who will immediately comprehend your beef. Mum. She takes the subliminal cue brilliantly and you remind yourself to post a nomination for *Mother of the Year* after all this. It's short lived when you recall she had one job to do regarding the birth of her Grandson and drank that opportunity away. Mum's out again. No mercy! She can take it and is proving most helpful as she redirects the staff and gives you some non-doggy-style space.

They shuffle over to the cack-festival of Green Man who up until this point has been a willow wisp of the sludge green variety. You haven't seen much of his eyeballs in the last few hours, but at least he's there in body. Conveniently for him the frequency of your contractions have been a nice distraction from his urge to purge. He either stands near you like a sweating corpse, or sits nearby with his head between his hands. He is never far away. Despite his semi-no show you are still sympathetic to Green Man's state – until now.

As he morphs from green to marble grey, the Midwives scurry about him. You rub your eyes. They rub his back. For a short moment your pain is secondary to disbelief. You watch on as the Midwives lean in gently and whisper something soothing in his ear. He manages a nod and they all cluck about him like a wounded chick and BOOM! Happy hormones well and truly disappeared. You will him to look at you, but he knows you too well and refuses to make eye contact.

Please let him look at me... contraction... *one look is all I need...* contraction... Your fury gets you through this one. Just as you locate objects to hurl Juliette comes back with a tray and your heat pack. You consider launching it, but are excited for Juliette's offerings.

Finally! Drugs!! Let's get stabbing! You incorrectly presume she's brought a magical smorgasbord of pain-relieving delights. She has not and you watch on mid-agony as the beautiful Midwife-in-training rushes not to your side, but detours to Green Man. Brighid pulls a chair up for his legs and they give him a blanket. He smiles like a fully grown mollycoddled man-child. You rub your eyes again.

This cannot be real. Is it the gas?

Unfortunately not and even more devastating – the tray is void of anything resembling a temporary fix for your ailments. Instead, it houses a breakfast banquet for the hideous husband mess. Toast, hot chocolate and a piping coffee. Threshold officially breached.

"ARE YOU FCKING SERIOUS," you yell out and the Midwives giggle even louder.

"We thought we better sober him up for you, lovey. For the main event!"

"Bring him closer. I'll sober him up real fast," you say like a mob boss from the twenties and oh how they laugh and laugh. Your Mum looks over and knows you're not remotely joking. You catch her *calm down love* face and serve her up a slice too.

"What's it for you then, Mum? Tea and scones?"

"Just the coffee, petal."

"I'll *petal* you, woman," you hurl and just as you are about to unleash your wrath on the entire room another wave smashes. This one is a biggie and it friggen hurts. You don't wail or scream throughout the labour, but you do cry a lot and the blubbery crocodile tears fall freely now. To their credit – your Mum necks the coffee, Green Man shovels his banquet and within seconds they are both by your side bear hugging you with their breakfast breaths. You cry some more, but these are tears of love and gratitude. They step aside for the angel Midwives who gently lift up the gown to do their thing.

"Time to push, lovey. Come on now. We'll be with you all the way." Brighid's voice is the guiding sound you follow when everything seems like an out-of-body experience. The mere presence of Juliette is like a soft bed of daisies that calmly supports your tired, weary body. They guide you in the most tender, warm manner and yet manage to retain your focus.

"I don't think I can do it," you whimper.

"Oh yes you can, honey," says Brighid.

"Of course you can," Juliette whispers and weaves the wayward strands of hair behind your ear. Every moment with them is a gift and even though the pain is bloody strong, you feel safe in the care of these two exceptional and amazing women. They never stop believing in you. Right until the very end they give everything of themselves and you will never, ever forget their selfless love and encouragement for someone they didn't even know.

The exhausted anaesthetist finally arrives with a bagful of apologies and a twitching eyeball. You've never been so happy to see someone so unhinged.

"Okay, Mrs Man. You will need to sit very still."

"I'll be as still as the grave," you reply way too enthusiastically. He explains the ins and outs of what he is about to do and you stare wondering why the almighty needle hasn't already been shoved into your spine. Less talk more stab.

"Mrs Man?" he repeats.

"Yep, get on with it… I mean – yes, I got it," you answer impatiently. *Just effing bring it! Bring that shit on now!*

He scowls like he heard and gently steadies your exposed back. You have never been so still in your life. You have no recollection of how it felt, or how quickly it kicked in, though the first try was apparently a fail-fest. Thankfully, after a few more rounds the pain waves disappear... for a bit.

Soon the pushing show kicks off in relatively pain-free bliss. You push and you push and you push. You do everything you're told to do, but this child just will not come out. A specialist of some sort comes in and inspects. It appears trapeze baby has turned and is facing the wrong way. After watching the caesarean train toot past the corridor for nearly twenty hours it looks like you're about to jump on board. Brighid comes over and rubs your arm soothingly and it's blubbering all-round. You know what it means.

"Naw, lovey. Ye've been pushin' and pushin' for hours. Best we hand you over now. You're a strong lass. You'll do fine."

"I don't think I am," you say. You mean it. In one of the most beautiful acts you will ever recall between strangers – Brighid kisses you on the forehead and the three of you embrace, sobbing together. You so dearly wanted these beautiful souls to deliver your child and lament this moment that was stolen by something as trivial as a pelvis.

This sucks. Time for a game.

CALL IT:
A) HEADS – CAESAREAN: PAGE 12
B) TAILS – C-SECTION MIRACLE: PAGE 79

PAGE 108:
A) CHILD FREE BESTIES

(from page 44)

It's a funny thing to look back and recall yourself before kids. It's even funnier to remember friends and especially drinking buddies. When you make your pregnancy announcement everyone is ecstatic. But, ever so slowly the dynamics of your peer groups start to change. You hang out less at the car park with the smoking rebels and more in the staff room with the old ducks swapping remedies for bum-nuts and shredded vaginas.

Before your little bean sprout takes up residency, your body has been on a decade long boozing binge-a-thon. If there was an actual profession for social drinking you'd be employee of the month every month. Nothing forges solid foundations in the workplace better than keeping your liquor down without yacking over fellow colleagues. Boy, could you put on a chunderless show. You were *that* drunk. A catatonic guest who provided free comic relief without the noxious follow through of vomit and disgrace. Alas, not everyone was a fan.

On news of the pregnancy Green Man was more than elated your drinking days would be shelved and naively hopeful the never-ending shenanigans of your pissy gal-pal-posse were over now that *Mothering* would become a priority (cue global cacophony of scoffing manic Mum's wine o'clock watching at 2:55 in the arvo, day three of the school holidays). Big ole NO to those high hopes. These chicks are your drinking tribe. A friendship connected by your intolerance of bullshit and embracement of everything funny. You've been searching for like-minded friends worthy of your madness since forever. Friends who don't deal in petty jealousies. Who know who they are. Who know who you *really* are and still love you for your witchy-poo lot. A crew akin to family and like the truest companions have no qualms in calling you out when you've lost your plotty-lot way. Friends whose main priority in social situations is piss-taking and joy until someone is choking or chucking from too much laughter. A tribe who dance with you under a full moon, liquored up to the eyeballs, wearing homemade tropical crowns pillaged from the lush hotel gardens and thrashing out to Balinese techno. Never discouraging your mad ideas when they probably should and always at the ready to defend one another with ferocious loyalty. These aren't mates you dump and run on. These are people you forge the most ridiculous life and death memories with. Bonds of sister and brotherhood that binds you to them whether you like it or not – forever. It would be an honour to rock on a porch of an old folk's home bitching and moaning about the food and drug portions, cackling about the 'good ole days'. This gang is bulletproof, or so you all thought.

In the magical world of Pre-Babyland there was nothing more irksome than soapbox parents chanting from their podiums to you childless peasants.

"Just wait until you have children... Things will be different... You'll see," they would smugly lecture. The waffling antagonists would be met with a collective *"Ugh!"* and you would all happily go home to a baby-free night of sound, silent sleep. What a fuss they would make. Of course the whole child-rearing thing would be a skip in the park for you quick learning experts (cue again wino Mums glee).

Unsurprisingly, you quickly learn the clichés are true. No matter how much experience you have, or how maternal you may be – something freaky happens when you have a kid. The love, the sacrifices, the responsibility, the genetic coding is all a beautiful and bizarre bit of woo-woo you will only know on procreating.

Childless-you was a naysayer who struggled to wrap your head around other people's parenting problems. *Like, how hard can it actually be* (winos hysterically choking now)? Those judgy years come back in a huge dose of medicinal reality. The next decade of being a piss-poor version of popular parenting hash-tags certainly gives you an education. You become a *#blessedmummy* of teeny, tiny, terrorists who test you by the minute. While wine o'clock becomes all-day-long o'clock mainly because of these chubby, hijacking additions – your sympathies toward other parents certainly evolves. When you do join the kid-club you confess your wrongness to the stratosphere.

Forgive me! I understand the eye twitch! I get why you remain silent as your kid hurls an iPad across the fruit and veg stand. You're just trying to keep your shit together! The desperation to shut this feral insanity down is the catalyst of surrendering like a hostage just so you can get out of a shopping centre unscathed! I understand now and I'm so sorryyyyy!

You all get it. Kids defo change your worldview in so many ways and though a few organs get a hammering – you look back fondly and appreciate the crazier moments of child-rearing. Eventually.

Your memories of the baby-free friends during this period are hazy. You know they were there for every milestone, every craving and every moment where support was needed. You remember the doughnut cake they organised for your last day of work. You remember the extra doughnuts that cake added to your cankles. You also remember the belly strap you had to wear to support your strained spine because of the doughnut cake consumption. It was worth it. That cake was shit-hot. Stacks on stacks of sexy little sugar holes of goodness. Mmm... yeah... lip licking lusciousness of bom chicka wah wahhh... HEY! Weirdo! Less doughnut porn – more lifelong golden friendship reflection.

You remember much love and laughs and temporarily leaving them to take the pregnant path that they too would jump on. For now, life shifts a little and that includes their grasp on the whole baby sphere you've found yourself in. You try to fight it, keeping up social appearances and insisting on wearing a wardrobe long past its appropriateness. But, you realise this road is just for you and the lacklustre Green Man and grow up a little... just a tiny bit, though you'll never not react to doughnuts like a four year-old.

So, while the support and comfort of child-free Bestie during the rather risky in-your-face-needle-of-uncertainty/amnio-horror-show is tempting – you are forced to reassess when she suggests calling past the local watering hole for a few inappropriate tequila shots before the appointment. Pressing pause on that liquor-laden life is probably for the best.

You lament your wild days for a moment, but the dream of finally becoming a Mum trumps all and you immediately perk up. Good news is you have Bestie with a baby who has had a gutsful and knows what you're about to go through.

Go grab her!

GO TO: PAGE 52

PAGE 109: SPRINT TO THE EXIT

(from page 68)

Well done. You made it out alive… *just*. You look back at the vortex that was, but Bestie shakes her head unnervingly and you pinky swear never to speak of the apocalyptic head fCk ever again. This proves a tad tougher at present as you both roll out looking like plump piñatas stuffed with all the things you didn't know you didn't need. You suddenly crave everything you can't have – a stiff drink with a side order of pate laden salami stuffed into a soft serve would defo do the trick. You salivate.

The eXpo was a lot to process with way too much attention to your lady bits. Bras that defy the laws of laws being hurtled at your chest and enough nipple cream samples to lube up for a decade.

"As if I'm going to need any of that crap," you naively spout.

Oh dear clueless one. You silly, silly potato.

GO TO: PAGE 85

PAGE 110: CHRISTMAS MORNING AND STILL NO BABY

(from page 15)

Christmas morning arrives with leaking breasts, the pain of a foreign body and no babe in your arms. You are so slumped you have to remind yourself to breathe. You stare blankly at the tree you insisted on buying for the arrival of your son. You stare and you stare immersing yourself into a cold and isolated space; a realm of nothingness. Of no feeling. Darkness. You quietly surrender to the indescribable sorrow and it feels as if your infant has actually died.

This is too flipping heavy. Time for a break.

Scroll down for some Nan relief.

TURN PAGE: INTERVAL

INTERVAL: CELEBRITY HEADS WITH NAN – OR AM I A CHOOK? (MENTAL HEALTH NAN-BREAK)

Nan is one of your favourite humans on earth. There is no better treat than to hang with her watching old movies, bad soapies or the footy while indulging in her stash of sweeties she thinks no one knows about that everyone knows about. She is the heart of your magical childhood and the world is sunnier, sillier and sweeter with her in it.

The oldest of ten and a natural nurturer – Nan ditched school and joined the workforce at an age industrial revolutionists would have questioned. In a shitty, dusty, hard-arsed era in an even shittier, dustier, hard-arsed mining town – the chances of becoming a charming stunner with a cheeky wit and an intact moral compass – were slim. But, Nan defied every turd thrown at her, walking through life with regal poise, albeit an accident prone one. She hands the gift of tripping on air down to you, along with one of her greatest characteristics – silliness. Affectionately nicknamed *Lucille* your Nan embodies the funny even when she doesn't mean to and **this** is one of her finest moments. A story so famous it has been passed down the generations and shared sooooo much – people who weren't even there know the tale off by heart. Enjoy.

WINTER – sometime in the eighties. A family gathering in the bone freezing hills where most normal folk would suffer hypothermia. Not you lot. Your Uncle had a habit of logging the fire so frequently, the lounge room was more like an indoor furnace. Everyone thought the kids were well behaved – they had just passed out from heat exhaustion. Much sweating, much hand-fan flapping, much clothes stripping. Family members would slink outside and stand in the frosty backyard until the sweet relief of icicles would form on their nose hairs. It was like a Swedish hot house minus the Nordic setting and birch whipping. To distract everyone from melting, Mum and Aunty struck up a game of celebrity heads. Everyone slapped their paper to their dripping foreheads. Nan was Mae West. After several rounds of her telling everyone who they were, the legend was born...

FAMILY: Okay, ask some questions ONLY about who YOU think you are.

NAN: Alright.

FAM: Yes, alright. Go.

NAN: Go where?

FAM: It's your turn. Ask a question.

NAN: Oh. Well, what do I ask?

FAM: Did we not just go through this?

NAN: I forget.

FAM: Oh, for goodness sakes. You ask a question that has a yes or no answer (*this instruction is no doubt where the confusion started*) like – do I act? Am I male? Can I sing? That sort of thing.

FAM: Okay, got it....

Long lapse of non-question-asking and relentless fire-stoking passes

FAM: Hello? Are you gonna ask something or not?

NAN: I'm thinkin'.

FAM: Can you think a bit quicker?

NAN: Righto. Do I act?

FAM: Yes.

NAN: Am I a male?

FAM: No and you *can* ask other questions.

NAN: Do I sing?

FAM: A little, yes.

NAN: Mmm, okay. So I act, I'm not a male and I sing, a little.

FAM: Yes.

NAN: Am I a chook?

FAM: (*pause of shock*) What? Are you a chook?

NAN: Yes, am I a chook?

FAM: How the hell did you get *am I a chook* from *yes you act and sing*?

NAN: Well, am I a duck?

FAM: Are you kidding? What's with the bloody animals?

NAN: I dunno.

FAM: Well, we certainly don't know either.

NAN: Well, who's doin' all the knowin' then?

Two and half hours of over-heated hysterics later and Nan still no comprehendy Celebrity Heady.

NAN: This is a stupid bloody game. Who was I then?

FAM: Mae West.

NAN: I was pretty close.

FAM: How?

NAN: Feathers. Dunno if they were chook feathers, but she wore 'em.

Nan. Keeping it real since 1929. Your love for her is limitless. She is the GOAT of grandmothers. #nanslegacy #amiachook #GOATNAN

(continued from PAGE 110)

Your Mum, bless her, handles things in the only way she knows how. Upbeat slogans, warm nurturing embraces and soldiering on with preparations as more and more family members file through the door. The house is bustling with joy, laughter and all the cheer that Christmas babies bring. With their rational thinking and non-sleep deprived minds, everyone knows this isn't remotely a tragedy and hug and kiss and love you with reassuring comfort. This is a time to rejoice! Of course they are right.

But, from the view of your shadows it all seems like the highest level of absurd bullshit. You can barely muster your usual veil –

Nod... smile... everything is fine... I'm okay... it's all good...

Not even for your Nan.

As much as you love and adore your family – this sombre version of you wishes they would leave you to your wallowing and shine their sunny frivolity somewhere else. Thankfully, you keep it to yourself, force an expression that may or may not pass as coping and praise the near extinct landline gods when the phone rings.

It's the hospital.

They need more milk.

Which you interpret as – *tests results are ready and you can take your son home.* You can't help but think this is like a Christmas courtesy call, even though you've long abandoned miracles. It's time to take action into your own hands. You are coming home with your child by any means necessary and if that includes getting arrested, so be it.

Getcha nunchucks ready badass. Shit is going down.

GO TO: PAGE 53

PAGE 111:
A) CALM

(from page 23)

Bedridden is boring. Time to check the *glow*. You've been waiting for this *glow* thing since you found out there was a *glow* thing and lend a hand to lure it out like it's some sort of mutation. You've been hanging for *Super **Glowy** Mummy* powers and eagerly open the makeup drawer that defies any logical order. You shovel gleefully through the madness until your hands look like a glitterpillar has died on them and then you find it.

Bronzer.

Time to *glow* with the flow. It could very well be the hormones, or the long absence of alcohol from your bloodstream, but even you know you've kind of lost it. You carry on any way and WOW – you are quite the bioluminescent organism and *glow* up a show like a deep sea monster with a bad fake tan.

Green Man walks in mid ***Glow**nation*.

"Oh, fCk me. What are you doing now?"

"Baiting the *glow* out."

"What? No! Just… not now. Why are you out of bed?"

"I told you – gettin' my *glow* on," you say matter-of-factly while busting out some electric boogaloo moves. He is unimpressed. You smile manically and continue painting yourself in what is probably severely toxic particles. He gently reaches for your arm, but quickly repels. He *glows* too now.

"My people welcome you," you announce and hold out both arms, cackling at your hilarity. Green Man is unamused.

"Why," he pleads more than questions.

"The glitter/bronze look was in when I used to go out."

"That was like a decade and a half ago."

"And? I'm still vibing it! Besides, this shit cost me a fortune!"

"Doesn't it go off," he questions frantically and rushes to the sink.

"I don't think so. I can't throw it away. I don't want the turtles to eat it."

"What?"

"The other fish might get bling envy," you share, far too seriously. Green Man draws a breath so deep, you fear he'll suck in half the furniture and you along with it. He exhales and reaches for your non-polluted hand, which he patiently kisses. You fall back in love with him for a sweet moment, but then he makes the catastrophic mistake of farting. *Glow* extraction is over and your insane reaction is on.

"Oh… shit! I'm sorry! I forgot! It just came out," he nervously splutters.

You have never been a fan of Green Man's farting, or anyone's really. The sound of the act itself isn't the big issue. It's more childhood scarring suffered at the hands of smelly bottomed kin who would heartily let rip just to smite you in some sort of rite of passage torture. You learned early on in life to accept the abrupt violation on your senses and in defiance trained yourself to become a champion holder. Even if it meant suffering crippling pain to avoid releasing a whiffle from the foofer valve region. Never in front of others. Because unlike your foul, flatulent family, the thought of someone hearing you, let alone smelling you, was too mortifying to consider. Green Man, however, subscribes to the *better out than in* theory, and the only difference between him and the percussionists who raised you – is the delivery of sound. His sphincter belts out a symphony that falls between the hornpipes and woodwind section of the big arse band. Non-preggo you could barely deal with it and pregnant you has minus zero tolerance. He was warned his guts' dropping ways would be met with a volatile response. Once your *super senses* kicked in he copped a pillow or two to his sleeping, farty head on more than one occasion. Beware the slumbering Mother-to-be choked awake by toxic tunes.

The ***glow*** is swiftly replaced by copper-hag persona.

"What did you want, anyway," you snarl behind a bronzed laden arm across your nose.

"Do you have any appointments coming up next week? I've got a conference I have to attend. I… can't get out of it… I tried."

"Sure you did. How come all these conferences are suddenly on your radar?"

"Ur… just my turn I guess." He fumbles like a see-through sack of bad excuses. You both stare at the other knowing full well he's actively put his name down for every lame task that eight months ago would not have been entertained. You're over it and your brain has already moved on to the bag of bullets you stashed in a shoebox in a poor effort to gain some control over your spiralling chocolate addiction.

"Fine. Whatever. I don't want to start an argument, but do you reckon you can do the baby room soon? At least the cot? We're running out of time."

"This weekend. I promise."

Yeah right, you think, but keep it to yourself now that stuffing your face is the only priority. He holds your hands and smooches them once more.

"You might want to look in the mirror before you head out, babe," he warns.

"You might want to have a look yourself, buddy," you respond. He makes his way to the bathroom and you waddle off to the kitchen leaving behind his string of profanities against the invention of bronzer.

GO TO: PAGE 80

PAGE 112: RETREAT THE BEASTS

(from page 55)

You gently pull the hospital blanket over your screaming she-hooters in the hopes you can ignore them. If a piece of material creates this amount of agony there is no way that monstrosity is getting close. But, like the rest of your spiteful body conspiring against you – tiny droplets of milk drip in protest through your nightie. *Deceitful bastards!* There's no getting around this.

GO TO: PAGE 24

PAGE 113:
WHY SUPERDICK? JUST WHY?

(from page 49)

No. No you do not. By day three it feels like you've washed down a handful of ecstasy with a bottle of vodka. You look completely off your head. Good news is everyone else looks just as crap. You reluctantly drag your hideous self to a Mother/infant/breastfeeding talk/session/thingy where all the Mums are holding their drooping faces in their knackered hands. You look at one another and collectively sigh that nobody has to pretend to be anything other than a tired mess.

Introductions are made, birth stories briefly swapped and then a moment of silence. Not an awkward one. You've all just zoned out to a mythical dimension where patients rest in soundproof pods and the planet runs smoothly because its birthers aren't half-crazed out of their minds from sleep deprivation.

Someone mentions "lack of sleep" and by gum does that release the whingeing flood gates. You all go in for a gripe then quickly conclude how silly the issue really is in the grand scheme of things. Everyone *Mummy* smiles and pats their empty tums. It's a lovely moment as the group bonds and chuckles over the experience in a relaxed, healthy manner. The quick vent gives you all a positive boost and a loveliness fills the air.

A few of the Dads have come along to offer support. They sit back and smile, acutely aware how the sweetness could turn sour at any second with the slightest of triggers. You smile back and feel safe within this group and all is one with the world – until one last couple arrives.

This birther looks absolutely corpsed-out munted. The midwife shares how she basically died during her ordeal. She barely makes eye contact and is one drop of drool off a lobotomised state. The group collectively nod sending subliminal empathy waves as she raises a finger nail of acknowledgement before slumping back into the chair. It's a cool, freaky-deaky vibe between a sisterhood of strangers that should have created a really powerful session.

Cue *Superdick* – the sabotaging partner who immediately puts everyone offside with his all-knowing enthusiasms and just plain old oddness. He seems to compensate for her lack of pulse, but in the worse possible way. The second he rocks up and speaks everyone moans. He heinously describes how the baby came into the world with every minute detail he captured and proceeds to overshare with the volume full bore. He fails to mention anything about the woman who did the work, instead prattles on about the most insane milestones his three-day-old child is supposedly achieving.

Now – *everyone* is for the Dads in the house and there is an unspoken respect and acknowledgement for them. No one is taking away the importance of their role, or the often forgotten supporters of what was formerly their partners – women who now occupy a hazy, painful and foreign post-birth sphere. However, *BREASTFEEDING, SUPPORT & SELF-CARE FOR THE NEW MOTHER* is what **this** session focuses on. You and the other Mums have hauled your exhausted trawls out from your underwater caves because **this** session specifically focuses on the *Mother*. The Midwife even says there are plenty of outlets that offer support to the Father, but seeing as it is the *Mother* who has just been brutalised – **this** is her moment for a little bit of learning, a little bit of support and a little bit of being fussed over. For the wellbeing of the infant the focus of **this** session is on the initial primary carer – the **Mother** and these Mothers are here for it. Like you, they've probably realised that when the healing is done and some sort of normality returns to your lives – those *fussed-over* days will rapidly be forgotten. You'll also learn that the more kids you have the more that fussing stuff will disappear like shit down an airplane flush hole – sucked out and disintegrated like it never was. So you're going to sucker all you can get from this.

Unfortunately, Green Man is working to pay off the million dollar hospital debt, which is a shame as he is often a calming force when it comes to volatile situations. You soon wish he was here and not just because you keep nodding off.

You look and feel like a squashed sandwich and the only reason you've left the bed is for some nurturing. The Nurses reassured you the session would be a brief one that wouldn't keep you from the bed too long and by the looks of the bedraggled company everyone has been given the same information. The group is grateful, as long as things don't drag out. No need to dick around. How complicated can caring for yourself be?

But slow cooked dick fricassee is on the menu today and *Superdick* is ladling a huge serving for himself and his *SUPER* unchecked ego. *Superdick* is going to BYO a podium, take things wayyyy off topic and drag shit out until he has pissed off every single person, including the infants – in the room.

Time to conjure your powers of suppression. This will be harder to ignore than a doodle shaped cape.

GO TO: PAGE 77

PAGE 114:
FINALLY BRING BUB HOME

(from page 53)

Green Man pulls onto the driveway and the entire family come out to greet the three of you. It's a monumental moment made way more dramatic by your lack of coping skills with stuff-all sleep. You blubber like a toddler. Everyone agrees there is colour in your cheeks and you look like your old sunny self. But you are not. The strain took its toll on a few nerves and it would take a while for you to resemble anything sunny. For now you, baby and Green Man are finally home and before you can walk through the door, your family are comically squabbling over who will hold him first. Bub – not Green Man. The authentic delight of each of them semi-mauling Mini Man and the outpouring of unconditional love for their kin is reward enough. Nonna, Pa, Granddaddy, Nan-Nan, Great Aunty, new Aunties, Uncles, Cousins, even the pooch gather round to grab a glimpse of this scrawny, slightly orange little berry boy and all are in love with him too. As you come into the beautifully decorated banquet room you can finally appreciate the elaborate spread your Mum and the fam have put on. Everyone feasts and much merriment is had as the Christmas you envisioned finally plays out even better with some of your wits returned. You enjoy the moment and make a wish on your Christmas cracker.

TIME.

Time when you and your son can finally be alone for days on end, catching up on the bonding you lost and never far from each other. Your wish is finally granted. Those first few months spent with your boy are beautiful and so, so magical. In a few years you'll remember that period and pine to go back every time you yell at him about his room, or his attitude, or any of the ridiculous shit you get worked up over. You get over it all when you see the first selfie pic of the two of you on the fridge. Those same big beautiful eyes that looked up at you on the birthing bed will always melt you to a smushy gooey puddle of Mummyness.

All the turmoil of the birth disappears when you nurse him, hold him, love him.

Those who endure storms

Cherish ever more the light

And warmth of the sun

And he is the sun. Your sun. Green Man's sun. A beaming ray that brings joy to all. A beautiful and special light who will forever deserve nothing but VIP seating to the very best of you. He was worth it all and you are so grateful he chose you.

THE END

OR...

JUST THE BLOODY LONG BEGINNING?

OR...

IF YOU DID NOT GIVE BIRTH TO A LITTLE MISS YET

GO TO: PAGE 94

... THE BLOODY LONG BEGINNING SETTLING INTO MOTHERHOOD AND THE NEW YOU

Good news! You get the hang of breastfeeding, eventually. With the *hiccups* of your birth experience it takes a while, but you and bub do find the boobie-boogie and sleeping rhythms. Yay! The drama of the previous weeks sink into the back of your mind where it slowly manifests into other issues. It's a long, complicated, bumpy road, but you do heal. It just takes a while.

For now there are plenty of other things that occupy your time and mind – of course your fresh new bub and the *new you*. What was formerly your body takes a little getting used to. Many say you'll get it back. You get something back you eventually learn to work with, but that pre-baby body? Kiss it goodbye. You ain't ever seeing that thing again. Welcome to elevated hip world and congrats – you are now a natural *Harry High-Panter*. Double yay!

Life keeps rolling out the funnies with the infamous pelvic floor and let's just say – you were warned. You keep the kegels up sporadically over the years, but big surprise – not enough. Kiss trampolining vigorously goodbye and beware the explosive sneeze. But, before all that hootenanny fannying fun-ness takes place – lucky, lucky you gets a free trip back to the hospital for one final hoorah of humiliation, because apparently you just didn't have enough.

It's a final checkup where yet another effervescent nurse gives you the once over. She prods around your middle, frowns then probes some more.

"Mmm. Ah. Okay. Oh, dear," she mumbles, suddenly looking at your hands. Your knuckle cracking is slightly anti-subtle.

"Put your hands here," she orders and shoves your fingers deep into what was formally your midriff.

"I don't feel anything," you say, hoping she's about to tell you of some freakish gene you possess where your body will naturally bounce back to a tight physique requiring minimal effort.

"Do you feel that gap between the two ribs? If you don't sort that out you'll end up with a weak core," she announces like she's reading out the lunch time specials. Shock! Horror! Another bedside mannerless human. You shrug like a zenny master of the *no-longer-gives-a-fCk dofu-discipline*. You recently graduated to a black belt.

"I don't know if I had much of a *core* to begin with," you attempt humour, but she's having none of it. She looks like someone who had first-class tickets to a luxury overseas resort and was called back into work just as she boarded the plane. She's vibing bitterness and is certainly not here for you and your piss-poor core gags.

"If you don't address it, it will become an issue down the track," she responds deadpan, or possibly just dead. There *was* a zombie attack recently, so who knows.

"What sort of issue," you ask, checking for sallow skin and decaying limbs.

"You can develop a flabby overhang across your belly that will be difficult to get rid of."

A fCking flabby what? You wonder if she uses this terminology for all the gals, or just potentially flabby you. Every conceivable bit of loose skin on your body currently flaps about like a flabby flag up an overhang pole. It can't get much worse than this.

"Is this like a health thing?"

"If you don't like a flabby overhang thing, yes," she snaps with no effort to disguise her snark. You're over being put down.

"It seems a little extreme. I only just gave birth."

"It's information you need to know so you are aware, that's all. You can tell which women take the advice and which ones don't," she states unapologetically with yet another horrible, soulless delivery that has you protectively hugging your empty tummy. She's just being plain old catty now and you've had enough sleep to know it's not in your head. What is with this place?

"Precautionary?"

"Yes. Exactly."

"The last time I took precautionary advice I wasn't allowed to take my baby home from here," you share with sadness and involuntarily shudder at the way too fresh memories. Again, you feel like you've done something wrong to someone who has clearly dealt with too many arseholes and her coping mechanism is to presume everyone is an arsehole. You are not an arsehole. You can be, but unlike true arseholes you always feel like an arsehole after the arsehole doing. Right now, you're just trying to keep it together. This is deflating and you're over being everyone else's popped balloon.

Green Man puts his hand on your shoulder. She hands you some pamphlets. Perhaps it's the repetitive psychotic drone of carols over the speakers that thaw her a little. She lowers her shield and gently pats your knee.

"Don't stress about it now. You *are* right. You've just had a baby. Don't leave it too long though. Try some exercises in a few months."

"Okay. Thank you," you say though part of you wants to scream *WAS THAT SO FCKING HARD?* You don't. At this point you are happy to take any niceties on offer. You don't need pity, just some kindness. It trumps all. Always.

On the ride home you flip through the info of what's in store in the little fun bag bonanza of childbearing aftermathness. The flubbery farm under your dress jiggles with every bump in the road and you find yourself feeling somewhat perturbed. The flabby overhang thing that may or may not present itself will be like a living trophy. The highest award displaying all that you've achieved – making a human! Sacrificing a flat stomach (that you never had anyway) in order to make a **life** seems a worthy cause to celebrate – not to flabby-overhang-shame. For now, it's the last thing on your mind as your potential overhang wobbles to the beat of the stereo like gloop on a subwoofer. The flab has some moves. #flabhastalent #overhang.me.sum.o.that

MUMMING

The first time round on the baby express everything is weird and amazing and surreal and emotional and exhausting and new. You can study, research and dissect every bit of info, every possible outcome and talk to every Mother on the planet, but no one will have the exact same experience as you. Shit hurts, stuff leaks, things bleed, and breakdowns can be frequent. But that baby lovin'? So deliciously sweet and just like a wand it magic's all that crap away with one nuzzle. Babies rule.

But, body reality is an actual pain in the arse, so let's start there. The bum bleeding is probably the biggest inconvenience you really weren't prepared for and the pain of the whole south region in general is at first quite severe. This is Mother Nature's fun way of saying *"You're healing well."* She is quite the jokester when it comes to the female reproductive system! Oh how we sisters laugh.

You have NO idea how people are up and functioning a few weeks after and will forever be in awe of those who do. You just want to shut yourself away and cocoon into baby world. The health nurse suggests joining a local Mothers' group, but the thought of sitting around swapping birth stories and having other people's kids crawling all over you, sounds a lot like work. You can barely tolerate your own thoughts let alone those of strangers with the only thing in common being birthing. At first you don't regret snubbing the Mothers' group thing one bit. But, eventually isolation and long stints alone are not a good mix, so of course Bestie insists you gate crash hers. These extraordinary females welcome you without question into their non-judgy arms. You enjoy many milestones with this awesome group of stellar women and share plenty of laughs, tears and boozy good times.

One sad, sad day one of the crew passes away without warning. You interacted with her only a handful of times, but every time was special and joy filled. For the greatest jibber-jabberers never short of conversation, the Mothers' group huddle like lost ducklings at her funeral – silent and in shock. There were signs she had attempted to share her tragic fate, but sadly you were all too busy dealing with your own lives to see between her subtle lines. It shines a blinding light on the relentless siren song most of us sing these days –

I'm just so busy…

Life is crazy, there's never enough time…

We'll catch up soon…

Can I take a raincheck?…

Whenever you saw her she would invite everyone to her farm and you eagerly promised to take up the offer. Sadly, you left it too late and she ran out of time. Another regret you throw on the pile. But, from this sad, sad affair comes a silver lining. The women you lost touch with re-forge the bond stronger than ever. They will always be your friends even when the babies that brought you together have long forgotten each other and the group gradually dwindles.

You are forever grateful you were Bestie's *Mothers' Group – Plus 1*.

As always – Bestie knows Best.

#melanomafuckingsucks

HOME LIFE

A few weeks in and the house looks like a giant baby clomped in and shat out the kid's section of Kmart. There is crap on every conceivable surface. Muslin cloths draped over the telly. Dummies in every nook and corner. The pump station next to the bed battles bottles of water, nip cream, baby books and milestone charts you foolishly think you'll keep on top of. You've got a notepad to record which tit you've emptied when and how long. When you are pregnant with your second child and find this *log book*, it'll have you laughing for an hour straight. It's up there with the Birth Plan.

The Moses crib next to your bed houses bubbikins who spends your downtime there, though he is never far from you. This is a sore point for Green Man who is over waking up in the middle of the night with an infant foot up his nostril.

"What was the point of me doing the room if he doesn't go in it?" he casually questions while you breastfeed after **F**-all sleep. Oh, the carnage. There are no words from you lately when it comes to idiocy. Much like talking clothes, you have developed subliminal-ninja-bitch-slapping moves and Green Man has copped a few metaphorical red cheeks of late. He launches at the comment to save himself from your barrage. You unclip a glare grenade and rain down one long, blinkless look.

"Na, you're right. Best he's near you while he's little and you have to feed him and… stuff," he offers.

"Yep. *And stuff*," you reply showing minimal mercy. It has been a full on year for Green Man and his self-inflicted stupidity, but he is unsurprisingly a great Dad. He rushes home from work, kisses you on the forehead and bundles up his Man-child. His favourite is to walk around the house in the fresh air talking gently into bub's ear and peppering his hairy little head with kisses. The poor dog does circus worthy tricks in the background in a vain attempt to get back an iota of his master's attention. Green Man is oblivious. He is in love with his son and it is one of the most beautiful things to witness, until you see the kitchen notice board. Green Man has chalked up an elaborate countdown for when sex is back on the cards with probability pie charts and tracking graphs. Of course he has. You may be sitting in the dark starving because reminders to pay the electricity and **milk, bread & eggs** have been erased – but penis goals are well taken care of. You've tried warning him it's like a spider web of the unknown down there and you are just as concerned for his manhood as you are for yourself. You tell him a little fable:

LITTLE FABLE FOR THE EAGER PENIS

In desperation to dip his wick, Uranus shoved his kids back into Gaia's womb – just so he could get some. This didn't sit very well with the Mother of Earth, so she took to her husband's testicles like turkey giblets. Chop chop. Hackety hack. Gaia hurled Uranus's goolies into the ocean and got on with the healing. From that salty, nurrie soup arose foam hottie – Aphrodite. Of course she did. Typical really.

Not that any of this ancient precautionary fable telling matters. Green Man appears to be patiently listening, but all he hears is "foam hottie" and adjusts his tackle accordingly. He is unbothered by butthole planets, or turkey testicle removal and ploughs forth in his quest for rumpy-pumpy.

One afternoon while lying exhausted from a restless baby night – you both stare vacantly at the telly. A couple are purchasing a home in some far off location you'll probably never afford to go to. Bub slumbers in the crib at the wrong time that will result in another out-of-whack night of minimal sleep, but everyone is happy for half an hour of peace. You sense something coming closer. It's got the lurch to it. It's Green Man's hand. You smirk and let it play out. You know the inevitable outcome he's about to endure.

In the background the couple view option two. The wife is complaining there is no dishwasher in a rickety old unit, in a third world country with a water shortage and a local uprising that could potentially explode at any moment, yet here she is bitching about white goods. Green Man goes to make his move, because nothing screams romance quite like watching house hunting shows in a bedroom that looks like an abandoned laundromat. He attempts a sensual fondle, but the nipple cream lather sends him sliding off the bed, crashing to the floor where he is greeted by an ice bucket filled with cabbage leaves.

"What the hell is this now," he asks dripping in gloom.

"For my boobs," you casually respond. He lies on the floor like a recently birthed goat and sighs. It's a *poor me* sigh. You're having none of it – not while your areolas feel like they've been doused in Tabasco and house three is on after the ads.

"We were using this for wine recently," he laments.

"Ten months ago to be exact."

"Guess that ship has sailed." The doom continues.

"While you're wallowing down there can you please throw some leaves up?" You offer little comfort. He rolls his eyes and lobs two bits of greenery as requested.

"I'm out," he announces un-goating himself.

"Did you actually think you were in? It's like a dead planet down there," you over share. It may seem harsh, but you feel worthy of not playing the ego stroking wife right now especially while you are in this amount of pain. Even though the thought of anything other than a cruciferous vegetable touching your chest makes you shudder – in the name of peace, you offer a breast branch.

"You can have a go. Just really, really, really gently."

"Pass." He grabs a pillow and exiles himself to the spare room.

"Don't you want to see which one they choose?"

"Three. I've seen it before."

"Well, aren't you a perky peach," you call, but he is gone leaving only the whiny woman who now complains about the lack of granite bench tops in the open aired yurt the whole village built just to accommodate these relentless first world fCkers. Seriously? What is with granite bench tops? People seem to lose their minds over them.

Regardless, your coleslaw party and Green Man's self-induced bedroom eviction has you irritated. Pregnant you would have been offended and probably balled at the rejection and lack of spoiler alerts. Not breastfeeding you. Breastfeeding you is a mammary monarch who suffers no fool. As much as you appreciate his struggles with this mammoth change, you are in the survival zone where zero shits are given about very little else outside the body/baby sphere. Boobs need tending, babies need rearing and as if to prove your point on cue a sudden stench fills the room. You change the bot of your little plucked chicken who tucks a beak into dinner and relieves some of the pain.

These precious seconds between you and your baby will be some of the most beautiful memories of your life. And whether bottle or boob you make a note to be as present as possible during these sweet bonding sessions that will be so short-lived. A minuscule moment in time you will always look back on fondly and miss dearly.

You make a note to offer a sympathetic ear to Green Man. That you really do appreciate it must suck for him at times and try hard not to drown him with all the Mum/bub/woman clichés – no matter how right and relevant they may be.

MIDWITCH 2ND STRIKES AGAIN
-OR-
ARE YOU EFFING SERIOUS?

Years later after the birth of your second child you come across the *midwitch* at another hospital. Yes. It seriously happens AGAIN and you ponder if you strangled a puppy in a past life to deserve this level of coincidence.

Without knocking, she waltzes in and you stop breathing. You feel sick. She has that same slow floating-across-the-floor-like-a-vampire walk and it immediately feels like you are back on that coleslaw cursed ward pleading your case,

"I'm sinister free! Let me take my baby home you horrible drama causing witch!"

It's deja vu all over again as she checks the chart and probes bub without acknowledging you, or saying a word. The sleep deprivation works in your favour. You pull the crib close. A surge of confidence stamps all fear of being a victim to this woman again. Not. This. Time. Mo. Fo.

"Do you remember me?"

"No."

"You were on the maternity ward when I had my son."

"Was I?"

"We were about to leave and you had him sent off for testing. I was a little upset."

"Really," she answers sarcastically, but you can tell she is curious, so you jog her memory a little more.

"You thought it was a *sinister* even though I kept telling you it was a scrape wound. It was a pretty horrible experience, actually."

"Mmm." She sounds bored.

"The results were negative, by the way."

"Lucky."

"Luck had nothing to do with it. ***You*** were wrong." Petty, yet satisfying mic droppage, but the *midwitch* smirks. She looks like she's enjoying herself. You know your pettiness may generate more negatives, but you cannot let it go. This woman heavily contributed to your long, long fall down a rabbit hole of mental unrest. A misdiagnosis that created a complicated, embarrassing situation for your family and a scar on your infant (which did not fade) that you will someday have to explain to your son. You're not after vengeance, but some sort of closure would be good – whether it's the cosmically correct thing to do or not. You press on.

"Do you work here now?" *Or do you just shift around the state spreading your doom wherever you go?*

"I'm with an agency," she replies, low and cold.

"Oh? How long have you been doing that for?"

"Around four years."

"Really? So you weren't a permanent staff there then?"

"No."

You laugh. Loudly. Here you were thinking she was some sort of authority. Is she even a midwife? *Nurse-witch* doesn't quite have the same ring to it. She walks back to the chart, but your tolerance for her presence is done. You do not want her spindly fingers anywhere near your baby.

"It was checked five minutes ago," you snap impatiently. She refuses to put it down and for a millisecond you panic, but thankfully your wonderful body sends you a painful bit of ammunition.

"Actually, I forgot to tell her I need another ice pack. Can you please get me one." It's not a request.

"You shouldn't need ice packs at this stage," she dares to say and you go to unleash a barrage of – *How do you know what stage I'm at? Are you and my nethers texting each other?* but maintain your self-control. Just.

"I know what my body needs and ***has***, thanks," you respond and retrieve a sad little ice pack from your house of horrors and dangle it toward the door. She stares back searching for signs of weakness, but is met with your icy glare. Without saying a word she slinks out as eerily as she entered, never to return. You are less than proud of your graceless behaviour and poorly justify it as self-defence. You consider making a formal complaint, but lack of sleep soon becomes your only priority.

Over the next few years you attempt to drink the entire experience away, squashing it deeper and deeper down. Sadly, you do so with such success you nearly lose yourself in the process. But that is a whole other series of books –

SO YOU ARE A BOOZE HOUND perhaps?

and

SO YOU ARE AN ANXIOUS AVOCADO

Maybe. Watch this space.

REUNION WITH THE WORLD'S BEST MIDWIFE
-OR-
THE GREATEST SILVER LINING OF ALL

A few years later you and Bestie visit a friend who had her baby at the same hospital as you. The deeper you enter the more the repressed memories bubble a little. Bestie takes you for a coffee at the cafeteria and you hear a familiar voice nearby. It's Brighid the Scottish birthing angel and one half of the beautiful Midwifery team who attempted to bring your son into the world. You approach her like a starry-eyed fan hopeful for an autograph. She has no idea who you are.

"Hi there. You won't remember me, but you were one of the Midwives at my son's birth." You gently accost her as she launches into a continental roll the size of a cruise ship.

"Oh, was I lovey? That's nice," Brighid responds between chews. You smile widely, flick a bit of pastrami off your cardi and put her out of her misery with your tale.

"You were on with a trainee. I was her final birth before she got her midwifery qualifications. You were both so beautiful and supportive to me and my family and you made the experience really lovely. It was my first birth and I was scared and weepy and you were having none of it. All I could hear was other women screaming and you coached me and made me focus. You helped me feel safe and in control and made me understand that giving birth was something to embrace rather than fear." You share this with her like you're both back in that room while she's making doggy style jokes and wiping your tears. Because you are an emotional drip you start to choke up causing the whole table of Midwives to put down their chow. Their faces light up and eight eyeballs are suddenly filled with joy. You can only presume that in this tiny speck of time you are shining the sun not only onto what Midwifery is, but where their true values lie. They collectively beam. Scotty turns to you.

"Oh, lovey! I'm so sorry I don't remember, but anyone who wants to tell me how wonderful I am is very welcome too!" She picks a bit of pickle from her teeth.

"That's okay. I didn't expect you to remember," you reassure her. She smiles even wider and turns boastfully to her peers.

"See! I am loved and appreciated by the masses! You have made my day darlin'! I get no respect from this lot," she says, her delicious accent much thicker without half a baguette muffling it. She cackles with such an energy that the entire cafeteria looks over and collectively make that smile when strangers catch another human's hilarity.

"She was clearly sedated," one of the giggling Midwives tease and winks at you.

"Shut up, you. Tell me more, dear girl."

"I filled in the feedback form and voted you *Midwife Of The Year*, but being a Mum took over and I never sent it in. I'm so sorry. But, you really were the best part of the experience and I've often thought about you both and always promised myself that if I ever came across you again I would be sure to say thank you. So… thank you! Thank you so much," you blurt and she smiles so wide you think her face will split in two. You want to cry. You want to tell her of the after-crapmath and how once you left her nurturing presence you were wheeled into a hell-like dimension you had not remotely recovered from. You want to put your head in her lap and be soothed by these maternal protectors as they stroke your hair back from your tear-stained face just as her and Juliette had done when you were at your most vulnerable. You don't. Why soil this moment by being a dibber-dobbing-tattletale? They do wear nappies after all.

She holds your hands, pauses the jokes and looks at you. She sees it. They all do. There is a nod of appreciation. There is a squeeze of *we get it.* There is an ancient camaraderie. It's a deep-rooted code of recognition. All the pain, sorrow and anguish. All the joy, kindness, love and truth. She doesn't even have kids, but she sees the lot. This is some kinetic sisterhood type shit and it is a few seconds of the most magnanimous empowerment you will ever experience. Everyone glows and none brighter than the beautiful Scot. She stands up, and even though she is the height of a six-year-old child, gives you the strongest hug filled with warmth and loving energy.

"You are most welcome and thank *you,* lovey. You really have made my day."

You float away with Bestie.

"Wow," she says picking her mouth up off the ground.

"I reckon. That was some woo-woo shit right there."

A WORD FROM GREEN MAN

YOU: So, what do you have to say for yourself?

GM: I regret nothing.

YOU: Ha. No one cares about your lack of regrets buddy. Howz about some accountability?

GM: I probably shouldn't have said the stuff about the baby juices.

YOU: Is that it?

GM: I don't remember much else.

YOU: That's kind of the point.

GM: Stop being dramatic. You were fine.

YOU: Was that before, or after I had to drive myself in?

GM: I may have overdone the drinking a bit.

YOU: No. Seriously. What else would you like to contribute to any of your dysfunctional efforts?

GM: You proved you can't be trusted with money…

YOU: Righto.

GM: I make really good green smoothies for them to get a mention…

YOU: Ay?

GM: … and you have no self-control when it comes to chocolate.

YOU: Seriously?

GM: I supported you way more than you make out I did.

YOU: I was more than generous with the shout-outs, and yes you came through when I needed you. But this is supposed to be your remorseful speech for being a drunken mess who was more worried about baby juices and car paint stripping than your wife in labour.

GM: Yeah true. I was a bit out of it. I'll probably never look at red wine the same again… or cabbage. You killed cabbage for me.

YOU: This is really heartfelt.

GM: … and I probably haven't been that sympathetic to the whole body issues you had. I didn't really know any of that.

YOU: Me shredding my clothes on the closet floor and crying *"I hate my body"* wasn't enough of a giveaway?

GM: I also probably could have been more relaxed about things…

YOU: Clinically dead?

GM: … and I shouldn't have been so concerned about having a kid…

YOU: You mean shitting your pants for nine months straight?

GM: … also I wasn't going out *that* much.

YOU: Oh, you were indeed, sir.

GM: Nah. You exaggerate.

YOU: Very much so, but I made sure the bits about you were mostly the cold hard truth.

GM: Me being '*average*' wasn't.

YOU: Maybe. The part about you being tall – definitely a stretch.

GM: We're the same height.

YOU: It's my story, mate.

GM: More like a fantasy.

YOU: Ha! Who the hell would want to live through that? If I'm gonna write a fantasy there'd be less hospital talk and more hot men feeding me grapes!

GM: Was there?

YOU: You'll never know.

GM: We got a beautiful son out of it.

YOU: Indeed we did, and a gorgeous daughter.

GM: Clearly my genes came into play.

YOU: Good grief. Let's just hope your brain genes come into play.

GM: Yeah. I'll be devo if they inherit your math capabilities, or lack of.

YOU: They clearly have my sense of humour.

GM: Tickets.

YOU: To our sideshow alley? Always.

GM: So that's it?

YOU: Unless you wanna go for number three?

GM: Not a fCking chance. I'll get you a dog.

YOU: And I shall hold you to that.

You did. The dog fits into the family like a thumb in a bum and like three quarters of your little unit – she is batshit bananas. Every now and then when Green Man is flicking the four hundred and seventy fifth dog turd off the deck, or sqeezing the putrid fishy bile from her arse glands – he occasionally regrets not following through with the third child. But, then one of the darling offspring screams bloody murder over a crusty old pen lid, or who owns a balloon stick minus the balloon, or goes full tirade over the injustice of salad, or chucks a ridiculous tanty over equally ridiculous shit for no sane reason at all. Green Man looks down the sphincter of your pooch and smiles. Well, you think he's smiling. Both of you have tea towels wrapped around your faces to prevent breathing in a mouthful of puppy puss. He muffles –

"Love the kids. Glad we got the dog."

CONGRATS YOU MADE IT TO THE END!
TO EXPECTANT MUMS & EVERYONE ELSE:

P lease don't freak out! Many, many, many people have perfectly normal, civil and average birth experiences every day. Try not to get too bogged down on horror stories. Mine was definitely an isolated situation and in the grand scheme of things – not that bad. But, if for whatever reason it's not a smooth journey please speak up and seek support. Suppression is the enemy.

I highly recommend writing. You don't need to be a writer (clearly) or intend to flip it into a tale for the world to read – but just releasing it from your system may help, as it did for me.

This is my story.

My experience.

One I've told many times to make people laugh. I hope it made you laugh. I hope it helped you relate. I hope it made you feel like you're not alone out there. It was written as a tool of therapy. It was designed to encourage laughter, support and an escape. I hope it generates healthy conversation and gives those who need it the opportunity to share their own stories both good and not so good and offer support in all its beautiful forms.

This is the part where I am supposed to encourage you to go to all the handles. There used to be a blog. It explained the multiple poetic licences taken as well as how the book came about, and other works that were (and still remain) in the pipeline. It really was a work of art. It had all the tricksy trimmings – witty little pieces and posts linking to perfect Pinterest images that steered you here, there and safely landing you back to the vomit inducing – "point of sale" page. But that lovingly crafted website is long gone, off to the stratosphere of a time when information wasn't so instant, entertaining, or demanding of raw as fck you-ness.

Then I'm to beg of your subscription/follow fingers on all the thousands of platform holder thingies that will no doubt come and go before this book sees the light of day. But do we really need to? Do you feel like the message of the book will be any different if you see my face and relate to me on some mythical social media level? I don't think so. And as much as my dream is to buy a cottage on a foresty hillside and while away the years writing – I'd rather forego the self-promo wankery in the hopes you'll buy more books I may or may not ever write. Instead, I'd rather you put your phone down, walk outside, look up at the sky and breathe. Go find a cool view. Even better find a body of water, shove your toes in the sand and sit your arse down to remember who you were, who you are and the resilient and glorious parent and human you will continue to be. I wish you a life without filters filled with nothing but laughter and purpose that will collectively lead us all to places powered by joy.

THANK YOU

THANK YOU

THANK YOU... for honouring my story your eyeballs.

Shine on

THANKS & ACKNOWLEDGEMENTS

GREEN MAN

Thank you for being my sacrificial comedy lamb. In your defence you were only really useless for the first few hours of my labour. Your Dad game has been strong ever since. You have lived up to and beyond being both a hands-on Father.

MAN CHILD

You are and always will be a beautiful light. I will always be here to help you shine. Never forget how amazing you are. The world needs souls like yours. You are the reason for this book, a tool that will make people smile and hopefully heal. Forever my sonshine x

BUMBALINA

You are and forever will be my gorgeous enigma. You tread like a warrior and I can't wait to have front row tickets to your future. My golden-haired Celtic lass. Thank you for dancing your way with inspirational grace into my life. Forever my wildchild x

NONNA & PA

Thank you for believing in me. Thank you for encouraging my writing. Thank you for encouraging me to embrace me. Thank you for being the most positive role model a daughter could ever need. No doubt you hear a lot of yourself coming off the pages. Always my muse. Always your permed haired, not-so-little, berry-disco-girl x

GRANDADDY

Not sure how you'll react to all this. I hope you see where your 'funny' genes come into play. Sorry you had no idea when to ring and not get your head bitten off. Thank you for being the Dad I always wanted. I hope I make you proud x

NANNY – THE BEAUTIFUL 'LUCILLE-AM-I-A-CHOOK-MAE-WEST'

The tiny amount of grace I have I owe to you. If I could be but a quarter of the kind lady you are and have always been – it will be a life well lived. But can you please lay off the sweeties? I want you to live until you are 120! I love you so much Nan. Thanks for inspiring me to live a sober and kinder life x

AUNTY

When I was five years old I knew I was destined to have children – because of you. I loved your babies like they were my own and watching you in your Mumming element was better than tv. Your presence during my pregnancy was one I am grateful for and your kind, nurturing nature has always been something I have admired and aspire to mirror x

BEAUTIFUL BESTIES

Unofficial Godmothers to my kids and my soul sisters. Thanx for being a part of my crazy story. I truly cannot wait to grow old with you my friends and to run a middle-aged-mok across the globe. Thank you for your patience, your love, your laughs and for never giving up on me xx

LEIA

Your words came at a time I was ready to pack it in. Thank you so much for your generous feedback. I truly am grateful x

BAKER GIRL

One sentence: "I burst into laughter hysterically in front of everyone while they gave me looks like I am a crazy person." You could quite possibly be one of the coolest people I know and if I could get someone as funny as you to piss themselves – I've already succeeded. Another heavenly sky-falling gift of a friend. Thank you x

MATT

Thank you for taking up the challenge at a moment in your life it was probably the last thing you needed, or had time to entertain. Your talent is unbelievable. I hope we can pull this thing off successfully just so your passion can be enjoyed by others. You guys are such goodies to be aligned with. Look forward to our future endeavours x

EVERYONE...

To every single person I have declined invites, offers, events, playdates, chats, greetings, not reciprocated favours, or seemed a down right snob to – please accept my apologies. This book consumed me. However, there was more at play. It took a year to learn how to write again, but it also took a year to live a life without alcohol. It took a year to re-acquaint myself with me. It took a year to figure out who the hell I am without a drink and how to do 'life' without one and not appear like a socially inadequate weirdo. I hope you can enjoy this sober, author version of on-the-run me x

FAN GIRL THANX

BEX WELLAR

Without your massive assist this book would still be in my boozy head. I will forever recommend you and your story to anyone who ever struggles with alcohol or finds themselves in the literal pickle I was in until I found your book A Happier Hour. Thank you a trillion times over beautiful angel x

BIO

STEPHANIE RAE – Average Mum with stories to tell

MATTHEW GARRITY – Cool Dad thrown into the random illustrating deep end

Neither have time for interesting bios

Instagram: @writerstephyrae

www.ingramcontent.com/pod-product-compliance
Lightning Source LLC
Chambersburg PA
CBHW020314010526
44107CB00054B/1836